GETTING EVEN WITH STEVEN

Original Story & Screenplay
By
Michael Selsman

McNae, Marlin & Mackenzie
BOOK AND PERIODICAL PUBLISHERS
GLASGOW   NEW YORK   LOS ANGELES
QUEENS ROAD, GLASGOW, LANARKSHIRE G42 8OO SCOTLAND

www.m3publishers.com

GETTING EVEN WITH STEVEN
Copyright © 2018 by Michael Selsman. All rights reserved.
Printed in the United States of America and in the United Kingdom by McNae, Marlin and MacKenzie, Ltd.
Except as permitted by the United States Copyright Act of 1976, no part of this publication may be reproduced, stored in a retrieval system or transmitted, in any form or by any means, electronic, mechanical, photocopying, recording, or otherwise without the prior written permission of the author or the publisher.

ISBN-13: 978-1-64316-119-8
ISBN-10: 1-64316-119-9

Reg: WGAW-1051705

michaelselsman@gmail.com

Visit us at www.m3publishers.com

GETTING EVEN WITH STEVEN

Original Story & Screenplay
By
Michael Selsman

Reg: WGA West
1051705

FADE IN:

EXT. DAY - HIGH UP ABOVE THE PACIFIC OCEAN

A rare clear day over Los Angeles, the mountains stand out in stark relief; the ocean sparkles in the sun, Catalina Island in the distance.

CAMERA pans down to the many boats passing up and down the coast and across the channel, and spots a speedboat racing toward Twin Harbors at Catalina's Isthmus.

SLOW ZOOM identifies a $150,000 SCARAB CIGARETTE just like the one George Bush and lots of drug dealers have; piloted by STEVEN GREEN, a good-looking man in his 40's in T-shirt and shorts. He takes care of himself.

Topless, and sunning herself next to him is a stunning BLACK-HAIRED GIRL in her early 20's. He motions to her to take over the wheel, which she does while he stands close behind her.

As she guides the powerboat over the waves, he indicates changes in direction by cupping her gorgeous breasts in his hands and leaning from side to side.

ZOOM BACK as the happy couple speed off.

CUT TO: EXT. NIGHT

THE MOTHER OF ALL SNOW STORMS

CAMERA is blinded by the intensity of the glare of the snowflakes; the wind moans.

We barely make out TWO FIGURES on skis, bundled against the cold, schussing right to the door of a luxurious condo in ski country. The woodcut logo above the door reads "Vail Meadows". They shake off their skis, stack them by the door and enter.

CUT TO: ENTRYWAY

Steven with another beauty, six feet tall in her stockings with long chestnut hair that looks like Secretariat's tail.

It must be terribly warm inside, because they can't get each other's clothes off fast enough. Nearly naked, and closer than Oscar Mayer and his Wiener, they sink to the floor just below camera range.

CUT TO:
LATER THAT NIGHT

Steven and the young lady seated in a steaming outdoor hot tub, bubbling away in the frigid air as the snow continues to fall lightly on them. They drink Roederer '69 and eat Skippy peanut butter out of the jar from each other's fingers, which they then lovingly lick....mmm…good to the last drop.

CUT TO: EXT. DAY

HIGHWAY ONE - North of San Simeon, on the way to Big Sur.

CAMERA is behind and trying hard to stay with a red $175,000 Ferrari Testarossa traveling way above the speed limit, hugging the curves around the spectacular Northern California coastline.

Waves CRASH against the rocks below as CAMERA, in an incredible feat of stunt driving, passes the Ferrari, and now looks back at the occupants;

Steven again, with ANOTHER beautiful YOUNG WOMAN, a luscious blonde who can't be more than 20, her classic features tell us she earns her living with that face. And as that face disappears beneath the dashboard, Steven jumps, grins.

A few moments and suddenly we rise sharply above the road and we're once again behind the racer as it gears down to corner into the driveway of Ventana Inn.

The Ferrari shudders to a halt in a spray of gravel. The two emerge, rearranging their clothes. She licks her lips, they kiss and go to check in.

DISSOLVE: EXT. NIGHT

A DESERTED OFFICE PLAZA PARKING LOT
Overhead fluorescent lights ghostly illuminate a beige ROLLS ROYCE convertible parking in a dark corner.

ANGLE ON A MAN, richly though casually dressed, furtively makes his way towards the building entrance; punches a night call button, is buzzed in and disappears into the lobby.

CUT TO: INT. - DOOR TO PHYLLIS STEEN, Ph.D.'s OFFICE

ON THE MAN'S BACK - He opens the door and enters.

Seated in a semi-circle, facing him, are FIVE WOMEN and ONE much YOUNGER MAN. He nods, takes a vacant chair.

Dr. STEEN, a chubby, raucously dressed Jewish momma in her 40's sits next to RITA, early 30's, zoftig but with an exceedingly pretty face.

To her left is KIM, a stunning Black woman. Then there's JENNIE, a short, slight heavily freckled blonde who looks like a young Doris Day. Next is HEIDI, a tall, well-built redhead and finally, TIMOTHY, early 20's, ruggedly handsome, muscular, bushy mustache. Everyone smiles warmly at Steven.

> DR. STEEN
> Everyone, please say hello to our newest member, Steven Green.

> OTHER MEMBERS
> (heartily)
> Yo ... hi ... hello, Steven!!!

Dr. Steen nods to HEIDI:

> HEIDI
> (stands, looks at Steven, licks her lips)
> My name is Heidi, and I'm a nymphomaniac. I've been dating my dentist. He's uglier than a barrel of hair, and I know I'm supposed to just say no, but I can't help it, he's just so sexy. When he says, "open wide," it's all over. I guess I'm just romantically humiliated.

> DR. STEEN
> Now now, Heidi, remember, self-esteem. Think of yourself as only suffering from a hairline fracture of your morality. There, now isn't that better?

> HEIDI
> Yes. And I took your advice, Dr. Steen, he's my first Jewish man.

> DR. STEEN
> Oh, and how do you know, by his name?

> HEIDI
> He's been circumscribed.

> TIMOTHY
> (suddenly interested)
> Circumscribed? You mean he has something written on it?

TIME DISSOLVE: As Steven considers the possibilities while listening to the other's stories.

> DR. STEEN
> Alright, Steven, it's your turn. Tell us about yourself.

ON STEVEN

                    STEVEN
          (stands, looks at Heidi, then around the room)
I shouldn't really be here, there's actually nothing wrong with
me. I mean, I'm not a sex addict. I just love women.
Independent women. It's so nice not to have to play games.
          (waits for reaction, there is none).
Actually, I like women who…aw, fuck. I can't think of
anything clever to say. I'm a serial entrepreneur when it comes
to women. I'm married, but I'm not a fanatic about it. I mean,
I love my wife. Even when she has her period, I just go with
the flow. But the only time I'm not thinking about having sex
is when I'm having sex. Yeah, I guess I got a problem.

The room erupts in cheers. Another round of "Yay…alright, Steven!!!" He looks at Heidi. She looks at him.

CUT TO:

INT. POLO LOUNGE - BEVERLY HILLS HOTEL - DAY

CAMERA hovers over the scene, cruising the busy tables filled with bizarre and interesting global types.

SWOOPS in, overhearing snatches of conversation. STOPS at table occupied by

STEVEN, who is huddled in intense conversation with his same-age best friend, and attorney, MIKE EMERSON.

                    MIKE
          I know your hair is supposed to grow faster when you're
          having a lot of sex, but when did you grow that mustache?
          You didn't have it when I saw you the day before yesterday.

                    STEVEN
                    (agitated)
          It's Magic Marker. Leslie drew it on me last night when I was
          asleep. It won't come off.

MIKE
(can't help laughing)
Leslie? C'mon, why'd she do that'

STEVEN
The usual…she caught me again. I was going to wear sandals today, but she also painted my toes red and I couldn't find the goddamned nail polish remover, which she probably hid.

MIKE
Don't blame Leslie because *you're* a pussy gangster. I thought you were cured. What about that 12-step sex addiction program you just graduated from?

STEVEN
That's where I met her.

MIKE
And how old was this one?

STEVEN
Uh…over 21…by a few days.

MIKE
Isn't that a bit young – even for you?

STEVEN
You're only as old as the girl you feel, remember that. Hey, I have a real condition; it's an addiction, like for coffee, or chocolate. It's called Satyriasis; it's the male version of Nymphomania. Don't laugh.

MIKE
I'm laughing because your "condition" is simply wanting to screw every woman you meet, period. That's *compulsion*.

                    STEVEN
My urologist said at my age I should have no less then four
orgasms a week.

                    MIKE
Yeah, I know, life used to be short and brutal – now, thanks to
modern medicine, it's long and brutal. Do you always believe
what doctors tell you? You're so dumb you could throw
yourself at the ground and miss.

                    STEVEN
This girl yesterday, she's just a kid. After we do it, she gets up
and watches cartoons. Cartoons! She's watching "Superman."
I thought *I* was Superman. (sighs) Don't grow up, Mike, it's
heartbreaking.

                    MIKE
I'll watch it. Anyway, that's why we're here. Leslie's lawyer
called me this morning. She wants out, and half of everything
you've worked your ass off for. But the worst part is the banks
will pull their financing and there go your plans to crash the
Asian markets. All those cute babes over there will be buying
someone else's cosmetics

                    STEVEN
She wouldn't do that...would she? Could she?

                    MIKE
She owns half the company, remember? That's what it cost
you the last time she caught you with your pants down. Or was
that the time before?

ANGLE

Almost elbow-to-elbow to Steven is an extremely striking androgynous BLACK
PERSON. Even seated, he /she/it is very tall, ebony-skinned, with impossibly
Large and perfect white teeth, heavily made up with exaggerated, high-arched
eyebrows and straightened black hair slicked back into a short ponytail.

The person wears a black and white checked pants suit, with a low cut Eisenhower jacket fastened at the bottom, and is bare-chested. Smallish breasts are suggested beneath the garment's line as it delicately sips its espresso.

CUT TO: MAITRE D' DESK

TWO BLONDE, fresh-faced YOUNG MEN in their early 20s enter and are shown to the only available table, right between Steven and Mike and the creature.

ANGLE on the boys.

Settling in, they look, then chatter together in a foreign language, probably German.

CUT TO:

MCU: Steven and Mike in mid-conversation, are stopped by their shared speculation about what happens next.

                STEVEN
What am I gonna' do?

                MIKE
You're going to get her back, that's what.

                STEVEN
Not this time. Sperm has a better chance. She threatened me with chemical castration if I cheated on her again. I don't understand why I just can't keep my dick off the street. I must have testosterone poisoning

                MIKE
Toxic cock syndrome is more like it.

ANGLE on boys.

A small Asian WAITRESS appears and the two young men in halting English order hot oatmeal, orange juice and coffee with honey.

MCU: Steven and Mike.

Steven looks at Mike and arches his eyebrows. Mike stifles a smile, looks down at his plate.

CU: The CREATURE'S EYES

Narrow as it observes the boys; takes another sip, then; stands, taking a few moments due to the closeness of the tables and its great height. From easily six foot-four, it leans down, looms over the two German boys;

> CREATURE
> (throatily)
> Would you kindly watch my things?

> HANS
> (stares)
> Uh, yes..of course.

> CREATURE
> (dreamily)
> Thanks ever so...

And totters on mid-size heels to the door and exits. After a few seconds, conversation in the room resumes.

MCU: Steven and Mike.

> STEVEN
> Flip you to follow it...see which bathroom it uses.

> MIKE
> This is serious, so listen. Say whatever you have to. She still loves you. Just don't pretend she's your mother and keep asking her to forgive you.

STEVEN
Well, what's wrong with that? A wife is supposed to be a lot of things to a man. Besides, if you had my mother, you'd look for a substitute too.

MIKE
Dottie is OK, she loaned you the money to start the company.

STEVEN
Yeah, and then turned on me when I married Leslie. You know what Attila the mom said to me yesterday? I asked her how she was feeling. Rotten, she said, looking for sympathy, as usual. I said "you'll outlive me, and she said, "I hope so." How do you like that?

MIKE
(smiles)
Didn't she also tell you to go out in life, find a hole and fill it? Stop whimpering and call Leslie. Suggest a nooner, be positive, be romantic.

STEVEN
(sighs)
B-Positive is my blood type, of which she's gonna' get half. Ok, I'll try.

He takes out his cell phone, dials a number.

INTERCUT

STEVEN
(false cheer)
Les, hi, it's me.

LESLIE, Steven's wife, 30ish, and a knockout.

LESLIE
Of course it is, dear. How are you feeling today?

                    STEVEN
Like shit. And I look like a transvestite, too.

                    LESLIE
I hope you wore a long sleeve shirt, dear. Those tattoos I drew all over you would get you arrested anywhere else but in Los Angeles.

                    STEVEN
Look, Leslie, we've got to talk. How about a nice quiet lunch together at the Polo Lounge, just you and me, like we used to.

                    LESLIE
Whatever for? So you can try to literally screw me out of my half of this company, and all the money we've made together? That's *together,* Steven. No. Not today, not ever.

                    STEVEN
OK, baby, you're right and I'm wrong, but we've got a problem. Mike says the banks won't lend if we're splitting up. You want this expansion as much as I do. It's what we've worked for for fifteen years. We can't let someone else take it away from us. C'mon, meet you there in fifteen minutes?

                    LESLIE
                (relenting)
My mother always said that one of the reasons I married you was because you could talk a dog off a meat truck. I used to admire that. OK, but no love stuff, that's over.

They hang up. Steven grins.

CAMERA roams the room; it must be Father's Day, there seems to be so many older men with their daughters. And isn't it a scandal the way young ladies dress these days, and in front of their fathers too.

CUT TO:

The entrance. All eyes follow The Creature returning; sinuously corkscrews itself back into its chair.

                        CREATURE
   Thank you, boys.

The German boys simultaneously stand, upsetting an orange juice, just missing Steven who hops to the other side of his chair.

                   HANS (and FRITZ)
                       (together)
   Oh, you're velcome ...

The boys scurry to mop up the juice. The creature moves closer to the boy's table and they are soon in head to head conversation.

A small COMMOTION as chairs and tables are pushed back. They get up at the same time. Hans drops a C-note on the table and the three form an impressive procession as they exit together. All eyes follow.

After a few moments, conversation RESUMES.

MCU: Steven and Mike

                        STEVEN
   Anvway, I'm cured. I'm never cheating on Leslie again.

                         MIKE
   Yeah, right. From the guy who thinks scruples is Russian money, and morals are what hang on the wall.

                        STEVEN
   No, I really mean it. I don't want to lose her. I love that woman, Mike. She's as responsible as I am for the success of our business. She's a great wife and a wonderful friend.

                    MIKE
                  (scoffs)
Yeah, I know. That's why you treat her like a baby treats a
diaper. And the second she leaves you, I'm gonna' be right in
her face. You don't deserve her!

                    STEVEN
Fuck you. She's not leaving me. She loves me as much as I
love her. No more strange pussy for me.

                    MIKE
As your friend and lawyer, Steven, I have to say you're a sick
man. My $400 an hour advice to you is to beg Leslie for
another chance, and for Godsakes, stay away from other
women.

Mike sneers, throws two Andy Jacksons on the table and leaves.

CUT TO:

Steven's POV:

LESLIE's arrival. She's tall, with a great figure. Maitre D' shows her to Steve's table.

                    STEVEN
                  (brightly)
Hello, beautiful.

                    LESLIE
                  (she frowns)
Don't you dare.

                    STEVEN
Right…sorry. You look great though.
                  (a moment)
I've missed you.

LESLIE
When was that, exactly? When your sick mind imagined a threesome?

STEVEN
(exasperated)
I give up ... I surrender, Les. You're right. I'm sick, and I'm sorry. I swear it'll never happen again. Never, never, never. You're the only woman who really turns me on. I shouldn't admit this, but (long pause)
I..I couldn't get an erection last night.

LESLIE
I 'm really sorry, dear. It's probably my fault. I must have misplaced your Viagra, along with my nail polish remover.

STEVEN
I knew it! How could you? You know how fragile my ego is.

LESLIE
How could *I*, you prick? Who do you think I am, Hillary Clinton? I'm taking your ass to the cleaners.

She gets up to leave. He stops her.

STEVEN
No, wait. It was just a flashback. It was like someone hit me on the head with a blonde instrument. I'll be good, just don't leave me…please?

She considers a moment, touched.

LESLIE
Don't grovel, Steven. I hate it when you're weak. I've already decided to give you one last chance, and I mean it this time. I talked to my attorney and asked her to hold off filing divorce papers – for the moment.

Steven's POV:

At that precise moment, a GORGEOUS YOUNG BEAUTY enters the room. Remember Bo Derek's first few frames in "10"? Steven's head snaps up, his eyes seem to bulge ever so slightly, his nostrils flare.

MCU: MIRANDA

Early 20's, prettily settles into her booth, arranging her long blonde hair, adjusts her spaghetti shoulder straps, sets her large straw bag next to her, ignores the hungry looks from the Japanese, German, British, Iranian and local guys.

Steven fumbles with his napkin, drops it to the floor.

                STEVEN
    Oh, sorry, 'scuse me.

He bends down, looks through Leslie's legs to Miranda's slightly parted legs. Straightening up, he bangs his head on the table. There's a thin film of sweat on his upper lip.

                LESLIE
              (concerned)
    Goodness, dear, are you alright? I think we ought to go home
    for a while.
              (a lascivious smile)
    What you need is a good tongue-lashing. And, I've just
    remembered where I hid your erector set. Meet you at home in
    10.

She gets up, leaves. Steven barely notices.

CUT TO:

Steven stands, begins approaching Miranda.

CUT TO:

MED: MIRANDA

> MIRANDA
> (to waitress)
> Orange juice and a toasted English, please.

She digs in her purse, brings out a large packet of vitamins.

CUT TO:

Steven - the hunter. Approaching from her blind side, reconnoitering, checking his position;

INSERT HIS POV

He spots her bag partially protruding into the aisle.

BACK ON HIM

Passing her table, he "trips" over her bag, crashing heavily and noisily to the floor, causing a small commotion.

Maitre D', waitress rush to his aide, Miranda is at his side;

> MIRANDA
> Are you hurt? Oh my goodness, I'm so sorry. Are you alright?

> STEVEN
> (groans a little)
> It's my tennis elbow. I guess I won't be playing for awhile.

He gets up painfully, rubbing his elbow, slides into the booth beside her, assuring the staff he's OK. He sips her water.

INTERCUT

> MIRANDA
> I just didn't think ....

STEVEN
It's OK. I'm clumsy…fell out of my highchair a lot. I'm Steven Green.

MIRANDA
Miranda Reed.

STEVEN
I have to talk to you but I don't have time right now. Here's my card, call me. It's very important.

MIRANDA
Why should I call you?
        (looks at card)
Hmm. Was that woman your wife?

STEVEN
Uh, yes, very perceptive of you, but we're divorced. I mean we're getting divorced. We were talking about who gets what. I'm very rich.
        (looks at his watch).
Listen, I have to run...

MIRANDA
Don't you think you should wait until the body is cold?

STEVEN
It's cold. I mean we haven't had sex in a long time…years.

MIRANDA
        (dubious)
Well, maybe. How many wives have you had?

STEVEN
        (grins)
In addition to my own?

Over his shoulder as Steven beelines it for the door:

>STEVEN
>Don't forget ... call me. It's about business. I'll be waiting.

CUT TO:

EXT: DAY

Driveway of Green MANSION in Bel-Air. Steven drives up in his Rolls, just behind Leslie, in her Jaguar. They exit cars and enter house.

INT. HOUSE

As they enter, a yippy orange toy POODLE attacks him, tearing at his cuff, growling.

>LESLIE
>Now, Rush Limbaugh, you stop that. Come here.

Poodle lets go of Steven, leaps into Leslie's arms, licks her face.

>LESLIE (con't.)
>He'll be OK now. I'll show you where your pills are and then shower.

She puts dog down and heads toward the kitchen. Steven follows her and the dog follows him, leaping up and biting his ass.

>STEVEN
>(slapping the dog down)
>Ow, ow...stop that! Damnit. One day I'm gonna' feed you to the coyotes.

Stopping at the $5,000 built-in Sub-Zero, she opens the freezer.

INSERT:

Her hand fishes among the ice cubes, finds his chilled RX bottle, hands it to him.

                              LESLIE
           Here, put this between your legs and rub them together like a
           cricket. When I smell hair burning, I'll be ready.
CUT TO:

Upstairs BATHROOM. An open (no door) shower for two or more. A large, green, slate-tiled area a step down from the floor. Six showerheads line the wall from overhead to below waist.

CAMERA POV

Leslie showering; and now we see what a fool Steven is for chasing after other women when he already has such a splendid example of femininity.

VARIOUS ANGLES

We observe her gently making love to her body, lathering, rinsing, and then drying. Although Miranda is younger, firmer, she is only a girl and in no way could compete with a woman so fully evolved. For a real man there would be no comparison.

ON Steven's hungry look;

Leslie glides toward him, toweling her hair. Doesn't look as though Viagra will be an issue. She slips into bed. He gets on top, when the poodle leaps up - and bites his ass again.

CUT TO:

INT. Steven's OFFICE – LATER THAT DAY

 On executive floor of Ariadne Cosmetics. It's oval, and seems to be patterned after the more famous one in the White House.

Steven paces back and forth. He picks up the intercom;

STEVEN
Has anyone called me?

ON DIANE, Steven's secretary. Statuesque, a slightly older version of Leslie.

INTERCUT:

DIANE
(verging on exasperation)
No, Mr. Green, not in the last five minutes.

STEVEN
You sure? It's very important. It's a woman ...a very important woman.

DIANE
(under her breath, *aren't they all,* then, to him)
I understand, Mr. Green. I've cancelled my lunch plans just so I can be here when she calls.

STEVEN
(ooh, good, he hates being alone)
Thank you, Dianne.

He resumes pacing. Phone RINGS. He jumps, picks it up.

STEVEN
Finally, it's you. Where have you been?

INTERCUT:

LESLIE
Why, right next door, dear. Did you forget we *both* run this company?

STEVEN
(quick recovery)
No, 'course not. I was just expecting the travel agent. I'm jumpy about the trip. I need shots, they got mosquitos there that eat your brain.

LESLIE
Well, don't worry, darling. Everything will be just like you left it when you return. I just wanted you to look at the Asian advertising campaign we've worked up.

STEVEN
Sure, sure. Give me a few minutes and I'll come in. By the way, did you talk to your lawyer? Tell her divorce is off, that we're back together?

LESLIE
Yes, I did, dear. She said you'd probably do it again, and that after we enter the Asian market, both of us will be able to take even *more* money from you.

She hangs up. That familiar moist film on his upper lip is back.

He picks up intercom to Dianne

STEVEN
Did ...

Diane cuts him off;

DIANE
Why, yes, a "Miranda" something, while you were talking to Mrs. Green.

STEVEN
(losing it)
Number...did she leave a number?

DIANE
(enjoying it)
I think so…where did I put it, honestly, my desk.. I've just got to get some time off.

STEVEN
You can take time off when I'm away...did you find the number?

She's had it all the time.

DIANE
Oh, here it is.

INSERT:

His hand, shaking as he writes it down ... and again, crossing out numbers as Diane repeats it.

STEVEN
OK, got it.

Hangs up. Then, picks up intercom again.

STEVEN
Diane, I'm going to the bathroom. I'll be a few minutes.

DIANE
Yes, Mr. Green. Should I notify Mrs. Green?

STEVEN
(panicked)
No...Why? I mean, why would you do that? I don't tell her at home when I'm going to the bathroom.

DIANE
(She can hardly keep it together)
I meant for the advertising presentation.

> STEVEN
>
> Oh. Yes. OK. I mean no. Don't tell her anything. I'll let you know when I'm done...I mean when I'm finished.

> DIANE
> (pinching herself)
>
> Yes, Mr. Green.

Back to Steven. He takes cell phone off his belt, dashes into his private bathroom, slams door. Dials madly but keeps getting it wrong.

> STEVEN
> (muttering to himself)
>
> Goddamn tiny Chinese buttons.

Nothing happens. He bangs phone on wall, battery cover flies off.

> STEVEN
>
> Shit! Fuck! Shit!

His bathroom, although lushly appointed, is small. He bends down to pick up antennae and bangs his head on the sink.

> STEVEN
>
> Ow!...(then, pain begins to radiate) OW..OW!!

Takes a deep breath, gains control, tries again. Success.

> STEVEN (con't.)
>
> Hello, is this Miranda?

INTERCUT:

> MIRANDA
>
> Yes. Miranda Reed. Who is this?

STEVEN
Steven Green.
          (silence)
From the Polo Lounge. Remember? Yesterday? I'm getting divorced!

MIRANDA
Oh, yes. How could I forget? What can I do for you?

STEVEN
It's more what I can do for you
          (admiringly)
Are you a model, you're so beautiful?

MIRANDA
Uh, oh. Listen, Steven, please believe me when I say I've heard everything. And you're a producer, no doubt.

STEVEN
Not at all. I'm in the cosmetics business. I own Ariadne cosmetics.

MIRANDA
You do...mmm..my brand.

STEVEN
I thought so, from the way you looked. And smelled.

MIRANDA
Well, I approve of your company's business ethics. I'm against animal testing. And what's your next discovery?

STEVEN
It's a trade secret, but somehow I feel I can trust you. (conspiratorially, into phone) Can I?...trust you?

MIRANDA
(just as secretive, whispers into phone)
If not me, who?

STEVEN
(he almost swoons, he's so in love)
OK, here goes. I'm on my way to Africa on Thursday.

MIRANDA
(flares)
You better not tell me you're going to slay some poor defenseless animal.

STEVEN
No, no.
(lowers his voice)
My scientists have discovered that Elephant sperm prevents wrinkles. I'm off to tie up the market... assure a steady supply for a new face cream we're developing.

MIRANDA
(eyes wide)
I guess I *hadn't* heard everything! Doesn't seem to work for elephants, though.

STEVEN
Well, it might if they put it on their faces. I called to ask if you'd like to come with me?

MIRANDA
I've been there seven times. And, you're right, I am a model. Africa's my most favorite place. When they're not shooting me, I'm in the bush. I'm hoping someday to do research, like those Gorilla ladies.

STEVEN
(barely able to control his excitement)
So you'll go? It's only for a few days.

                    MIRANDA
You got lucky, Mr. Green. It's the only thing you could have
said that could get me. It won't be long before the real Africa
is gone. I want to experience as much of it as I can before it is.

                    STEVEN
Meet me at Air India, 10 am sharp Thursday.

                    MIRANDA
Done, and oh, how are you going to persuade those big bull
elephants to part with their sperm?

                    STEVEN
               (that stops him for a moment)
I don't know.
               (then, a grin)
Maybe that could be your first research project.

He hangs up. Leaves bathroom, then, dashes back in, flushes toilet. Jauntily, he walks through his office, stops in front of Diane's desk.

                    STEVEN
               (full of confidence, like he's just shot up in there)
I'll be in Leslie's office. For the advertising presentation.

ANGLE

He enters Leslie's equally beautiful office.

WIDE

We see a group: Leslie, LISA, their AD MANAGER, several other FEMALE EXECS from the agency, and assorted help. A projector and screen is set up. Around the room are easels with large, colorful ad mock-ups.

INTROS all around.

                    LESLIE
                  (to group)
    We can begin now that Steven's here. (then, to Steven)
    Oh, by the way, Steven, I have good news. I managed to clear
    my schedule and I'm coming on the African trip with you after
    all.

On his STRICKEN face, CUT TO:

INT. HOLLAND & HOLLAND

Steven, being fitted for the very latest in up-scale safari ware. The salesman is between his legs, measuring his in-seam.

ANGLE - Leslie looks on critically.

ANOTHER ANGLE

A stack of bush pants/jackets, shirts, boots and two white hunter hats are piled up at the cash register. Leslie settles up as Steven throws a spray can of mosquito repellent into the bag.

POV:

They exit, arms around each other. A great marriage, once more. Or so it seems.

CUT TO:

INT. Green BEDROOM.

Steven packs. He stops to admire himself in full-length mirror wearing his new duds, especially his hat. Stewart Granger he's not.

INT. Leslie's bathroom.

She's rummaging through drawer - finds what she's looking for, a bottle of blue DULCOLAX pills for constipation.

INSERT:

She empties Steven's Viagra bottle, replacing them with the Dulcolax, then caps it. Thinking a second, she re-opens the bottle and puts a couple of Viagra pills back, shaking the bottle to mix them up. She exits into bedroom.

ON Steven - still admiring himself.

> STEVEN
> Don't you ever die!

She hands him the pill bottle. He tosses it offhand into his carry-on. Leslie leaves. Steven grabs the bottle, holds it up to the light, mentally counting. A dozen. Not enough. What to do? Leslie knows *exactly* how many there are.

He grabs his cell phone and dashes into the bathroom - hurriedly dialing.

> MIKE
> Hello?

> STEVEN
> It's me. I need your Viagra. Can you bring them right over?

> MIKE
> I knew you were nuts. Ask me anything ... for a kidney transplant, anything, but I'm not giving you my pills.

> STEVEN
> You're supposed to be my friend. I *need* them.

> MIKE
> I'm not gonna' feed your addiction. Besides, what am I gonna' do when *I* need them?

> STEVEN
> You haven't gotten laid since high school. C'mon, please. I'll raise your rates.

>   MIKE
>   I'll be there in fifteen minutes.

CUT TO:

THURSDAY, early A.M., Day of the trip.

Leslie is showering. Steven is ready to go, but he has a problem.

>   STEVEN
>   (to himself)
>   She must not go ... she can not go. There has to be some way
>   of keeping Leslie off that plane.

Then, an idea!

>   STEVEN (con't.)
>   Yes!

CUT TO:

The noise of Leslie's shower masks Steven's entry into her bathroom. Sneaking in like Anthony Perkins on Janet Leigh, he quietly opens her medicine cabinet, doesn't find what he's looking for. Stealthily, he opens drawer - bingo! The Dulcolax pills. The bottle is almost empty. He takes the remaining three and steals away.

INSERT: Phone rings. Steven picks it up.

>   STEVEN
>   Hello?

INSERT:

Limo DRIVER at front gate.

> DRIVER
> Larry Flynt Limo Service.

> STEVEN
> Who? Larry Flynt has a limo service?

> DRIVER
> That's right. Diane from your office booked it.

> STEVEN
> Oh, OK. We'll be down in about 20 minutes.

On his LOOK

CUT TO:

Steven's kitchen. He's got the pantry door open, searching....for what...there it is, peanut butter. Rush Limbaugh, their orange Poodle is tearing at his cuff.

> STEVEN
> (Jerking away)
> Shut up, you rat with fur.

INSERT:

Steven rolling the three constipation pills in peanut butter, feeding them to the dog.

> STEVEN
> Here, don't say I never gave you anything.

The dog gulps them down, licks his lips, looks up at Steven. Maybe that jerk isn't such a bad guy after all.

SOUNDS of shower stop. Steven looks around, goes to front door, switches gate open for limo.

WIDE on driveway.

When Larry Flynt is away, his LIMO is occasionally for rent. It's a block long, snow-white, black-windowed, with a huge painting of a naked woman on each side panel. Great advertising. Needless to say, Steven is wowed. Bad taste has never held him back.

CUT TO:

INT. Bedroom.

Leslie is dressed and ready. The limo driver has an armload of bags and is on his way downstairs. She grabs her carry-on and Steven does the same.

CUT TO:

Kitchen. The Poodle doesn't look too good. He's staggering in circles, his tongue lolling.

                      LESLIE
        Something's wrong with the dog.

                      STEVEN
        He's fine. C'mon, we gotta' go, we'll be late.

Just then, the dog lets go. All over the floor. Steven has to jump out of the way because Rush is spewing frantically. Good thing there's no fan nearby.

                      LESLIE
                      (panicked)
        OhmiGod! He's sick...he's dying. Rush...darling, what's
        wrong.

The dog looks daggers at Steven. He knows! He was right all the time.

Leslie grabs phone - stabs vet's speedcall digits.

                    LESLIE
Hello, this is Leslie Green. My dog's been poisoned!... no, I
don't know. Yes, he goes out sometimes. Gardeners? Yes, we
have gardeners. Snails? I don't know. Do what?

She reaches for pad and pencil, hurriedly scribbles.

                    LESLIE
Got it. Poison control Center, Washington, D.C.

Hangs up. Starts hurriedly dialing. The dog meanwhile, looks near death.

                    LESLIE
Hello, Poison Control Center? Yes, my dog's dying.
Transferring me? To whom?
          (to Steven)
Look, I can't go
          (back to Poison Center)
Goddamn it, push one if it's a horse?
          (back to Steven)
I'll get the next plane.

                    DRIVER
We've gotta' leave or we'll miss the flight.

                    STEVEN
OK, OK. Listen darling, I'll miss you. I hope Rush is OK.

The dog, dehydrated as he is, has just enough energy to raise his little head and glare at Steven, probably cursing him on every dog's behalf for 100,000 years of servitude.

                    LESLIE
I'll miss you too, darling. I'll text you every day.

CUT TO:

The limo on the 405. Steven in the back seat trying out all the gadgets, sniffing the contents of the bottles in the bar. Furtively speed-surfing the back issues of "Hustler" in the magazine rack.

INSERT:

Various shots of other drivers, speeding up to get alongside, straining to see into the opaque windows. Steven grins. This is fun.

INSERT:

Steven's POV:

Cruising past the limo, a 5-ton truck with a backhoe lashed to the bed. A logo on the truck's side reads *"Smitty's Backhoe – Your hole, our goal."*

Another grin – an omen?

CUT TO:

LAX

The limo pulls up to the curb in front of Air India.

ANGLE ON

Steven, dressed for Africa in his white hunter best and wearing his hat, jumps out as the trunk pops, turns his bags over to the curbside redcap. Other travelers gape.

CUT TO:

INT. PASSENGER WAITING AREA, Air India

INSERT CU: on wall clock; 10 a.m.

SPEAKERS BOOM:

> SPEAKERS
> All passengers. Air India flight 0018 to Karachi, Lagos and Djibouti is boarding at gate 61.

ANGLE

Steven, pacing nervously as the minutes tick by. Miranda is late...very late..what to do ... ?

Speakers AGAIN:

                SPEAKERS
Final boarding call - All passengers for Air India flight 0018.

CU: Steven, biting his nails.

CUT TO: STOCK

Through passenger lounge window; Air India 0018, backing away from gate.

CUT TO:

Steven, all alone.

IN B.G: PASSENGER AGENTS packing up, moving on.

ON Steven. He's in a funk, suddenly looks up:

CUT TO:

Steven's POV:

Miranda, running towards him, long blonde hair flying, sundress pressed against her lovely body, shoulder bag flapping.

CUT TO:

REVERSE: Miranda's dash...pulls up to Steven;

INTERCUT

                    MIRANDA
            (breathless, but beautiful)
    The traffic...and then my hair curler set off the metal
    detector..and..

                    STEVEN
            (very relieved)
    It's OK, Miranda ... I'm just glad you're here.
            (then, disappointed)
    We missed the plane, tho.

                    MIRANDA
    Oh, God .... I'm sorry.

She looks helpless, and dammit, too gorgeous to be angry at.

                    STEVEN
    And the next plane isn't until tomorrow. I guess we'll have to
    go home.

                    MIRANDA
    Why?...look, it's all my fault. I feel terrible, we're all packed
    and at the airport. Be a shame to waste it ... Let's go someplace
    else for a couple of days, then we'll go to Africa.

                    STEVEN
            (getting that familiar warm feeling down below)
    Sure...where?

                    MIRANDA
    I don't know...let's look.

She grabs his hand, pulling him down the corridor past other international airlines.

TRAVEL WITH THEM

Posters advertising exotic travel destinations line the walls:

TAHITI: She shakes her head. They continue walking;

> MIRANDA
> Too far...

THE HOLY LAND:

> MIRANDA (cont.)
> Not enough time ... want to see it, though.

MEXICO:

> MIRANDA (cont.)
> (excited)
> That's it ... Couple of hours. I know just the spot. Went on a shoot last year to a deserted island off the coast. Nobody there but us.

Steven is hanging on every word, already has his American Express card out. He can't wait.

> STEVEN
> (as they head toward the Aero Mexico counter)
> Sounds terrific. Mr. & Mrs. Robinson Crusoe. What about my luggage, it's on the plane – with my cell phone.

> MIRANDA
> You won't need it. C'mon.

CUT TO:

EXT. DAY. A DOCK jutting out into the OCEAN

Miranda, wearing Steven's white hunter hat, and a perspiring Steven wait in the hot sun, scanning the horizon outside a sleepy Mexican village.

THEIR POV:

In the distance a speck appears; rapidly becomes a small seaplane, a Grumman Goose, vintage 1940, its fabric skin heavily patched.

It plops down into the water and slowly taxies to the dock. Engines stop.

ANGLE ON

FRANKLEY, the pilot emerges;

Despite the heat, he wears a beat-up leather flying jacket, gloves and a WWII U.S. Air Force cap. He's in his late 60's at least and has probably been flying this heap since the war. Think Bogie in "African Queen".

                    FRANKLEY
        Howdy, pardners, I'm Frankley Truly. Got your call on my
        radiophone.

Steven and Miranda look at each other; he's concerned, she smiles.

                    MIRANDA
        Howdy, Frankley, remember me? I'm taking my friend to
        Tetoni Ladas island.

                    FRANKLEY
        (remembering, smiles..spits a long stream
          of tobacco juice at least 10 feet into the ocean)
        Got any U.S. cash? Don't want any damn pesos.

Miranda JABS Steven with her elbow.

                    STEVEN
        (wakes up from his staring)
        Oh, yeah..sure.

Digs in his pocket, pulls out a wad of greenbacks. Frankley looks hungrily at it.

                            FRANKLEY
            That'll be $500…each way. Hard to get parts for this baby.

He rests his weight on the fuselage and his hand goes right through one of the patches. He hurriedly pulls his hand out. Steven peels off five $100's and they pile into the plane.

Frankley stands, one foot on the dock, the other on the plane's float, shoves off. As his legs spread, he loses his grip and grabs onto the plane's struts for dear life.

The PLANE

The Goose floats free, drifts further from the dock and Frankley is in the drink.

ANGLE on Frankley.

Half drowned, he pulls himself onto the float and into the cramped cockpit, no larger inside than a Ford Taurus.

Steven, huddled with Miranda on jump seats just behind the pilot's seat is clearly worried.

                            FRANKLEY
                        (dripping onto controls)
                    Damn, that's cooling.

Firing up the two ancient engines in a great cloud of greasy smoke, nearly enveloping the plane, he taxies out into the ocean;

WIDE from dock.

Slowly, painfully gathering speed, the Goose lifts up and finally flies, no more than two hundred feet over the water.

Steven, although airsick, is nevertheless feeling better - a comforting and familiar bulge in his pants. Glancing at Miranda looking out her window, love overcomes him once more.

ANGLE past Frankley, through WINDSHIELD

A small ISLAND soon appears on the horizon, it's distinguishing feature two heavily foliaged hills; except for their peaks from which jut iron-rich pinkish mounds of rock. From the air, it's like looking down at a huge pair of breasts, hence the name the natives have given it, TETONI LADAS, "Ten-Ton Tits".

FRANKLEY puts the Goose into a STEEP DIVE.

ANGLE on Steven.

He GRIPS Miranda as they descend, seemingly to hit the surface, and to Steven's horror, they do!

He SCREAMS out as green water covers the plane's windows.

> STEVEN
> We're goners...Oh, God, I didn't have children!

> MIRANDA
> Hush up, silly...haven't you ever been in a seaplane before?

CUT TO:

EXT. the ocean.

The Goose pops up and floats, as it has for sixty years. Frankley GUNS the two overhead engines and ROARS toward the beach.

ON Steven, relieved, and very embarrassed.

CUT TO:

C.U: The Goose's wheels, which Frankley lowered during the dive, touch sand, spinning as they grip, hauling the plane onto the beach, engines HOWLING.

ON Frankley as he turns the Goose around facing the ocean again. He leans over, opens the door.

EXT.

THE BEACH

Steven and Miranda pile out.

BACK ON Frankley.

                FRANKLEY
           (grins, aside to Steven)
Well, boy, stop that grinnin' and drop yer' linen. Ya' know, some of these little gals, they get all titted up, ain't no tellin' just what they're gonna' do. (sighs)

EXT. Beach. Looks like they're the first humans ever to set foot on it.

                MIRANDA
           (yells out over the roaring engines)
Thank you, Frankley, lovely flight. Pick us up day after tomorrow.

HER POV

Frankley nods.

                FRANKLEY
           (calls out loudly)
And watch out for the coconuts.

He slams the door and heads the Goose out into the ocean.

POV from the beach:

Picking up speed, the little plane lifts off and fades away over the horizon.

                STEVEN
What the hell did he mean by that?

Miranda shrugs. Then,

> MIRANDA
> Oh, I forgot to mention it, but there's no McDonalds, or anything like that on this island. Just fruit off the trees, and some veggies.

> STEVEN
> (another leer, he can't help it)
> No problem. I'm a *vagiterian*.

On her LOOK

CUT TO: AERIAL

Steven and Miranda, two small figures on a very large and deserted beach.

POV:

The SUN is high overhead; aside from the crashing surf, the wind and an occasional seagull, they are alone.

Miranda drops her little bag and dashes down the beach, shedding her sandals and then her sundress. Other than her shell necklace, she is naked and even more beautiful than Steven in his wildest dreams had imagined. And now that he has what he wanted, he doesn't quite know what to do.

Shrugging, he rips off his safari shirt and charges after her, hopping and skipping as he tries to dump his pants as well.

FOLLOW HIM

By the time he catches up to her, he's wearing only his black bikini jockeys. He pulls up, out of breath; Miranda surveys him, and with a giggle, reaches down and pulls down his jockeys.

POV from his rear:

Red-faced, embarrassed, he's used to being in control. An instant decision as she begins to run again. He follows, ready for whatever adventure lies ahead.

WIDE

As Miranda lets him "catch" her, they crash to the sand, half in the surf, and nature takes its course. It's a commercial for hetero sex.

DISSOLVE:

EXT. Bel Air - Green home.

ANGLE - END of DRIVEWAY- DAY

ESMERALDA, the Green's housekeeper, retrieves the mail, examines the letters and magazines finds a small, strange box, crudely wrapped in brown paper, looks it over, returns through front door.

CUT TO:

INT. Bedroom.

MCU: Leslie is handed the box while having her massage. Curious, she unwraps it, finds Steven's college fraternity ring with a tightly wound piece of paper through it; signals JUNE, the masseuse to hold up a minute, scans the note.

Suddenly, CRYING OUT, she jumps up, momentarily revealing her sensational figure, alarming June and Esmeralda.

LESLIE
Oh, my God ... oh, my God ....

ESMERALDA
What it is, missiz.... ?

Leslie wraps the sheet around her and leaps off the table. To June:

LESLIE
June, I have to stop now. I'll call you.

June, concerned, begins to pack up.

                    LESLIE
            Oh, my God ...

She rushes into jeans, no undies, sneakers, no socks, and a T-shirt, no bra. The shirt clings to her lovely, heavily oiled body. Grabbing the phone she punches in a number and paces nervously, waiting for an answer.

                    LESLIE
            Diane ... Leslie Green ... listen, have you heard from Steven?

INTERCUT:
                    DIANE
                (Looks at her watch)
            No, Mrs. Green. He's not due in Lagos for another twelve hours.

                    LESLIE
            Find out if we can call the plane and call me back.

Hangs up, punches out another number, chewing on a fingernail.

                    LESLIE
            Michael Emerson, please. It's very important (pause), Leslie Green ... thank you, I'll wait.

She continues to pace, goes to bed, picks up note again, re-reads it.

                    LESLIE
            Oh, Mike...I must talk to you, it's urgent. No, not on the phone. Do you know of any other plans Steven may have made besides his African trip?

Listens.

                    LESLIE
            No, huh? OK, I'll you up in front of your building in 20 minutes.

Hangs up.

FOLLOW LESLIE AS SHE RACES downstairs, through the kitchen into the garage, Esmeralda right behind her as she gets behind the wheel of her Jag.

> LESLIE
> Esmeralda, stay by the telephone… take any messages very clearly, comprende? Yo telephono.

ON ESMERALDA as she nods, stands back.

POV - the Jag SHOOTS out of the garage and down the driveway, turning into the street, disappearing into traffic.

CUT TO:

INT. JAGUAR

Leslie, wearing big round shades, cell phone to her ear as she drives.

> LESLIE
> Answer, dammit ... Hello, Dottie? This is Leslie. Yes, I'm fine. Did Steven call you before he left town ... no, this trip. He didn't? So you don't know. OK, listen, I'm in a hurry.... what? No, I don't know if we're coming for dinner Friday night.... I'll call you later.

Hangs up and concentrates on her driving, WEAVING in and out of Sunset Blvd. traffic.

CUT TO: EXT. DAY

TETONI LADAS ISLAND - A picture postcard. The SUN is high.

CAMERA picks up two figures sitting on the sand; Steven and Miranda.

SLOW ZOOM IN

MIRANDA

Glad you came?

STEVEN
(grins)

Every time. Listen, I'm falling in love with you…and that worries me, because of our age difference. Will you still want to make love to me when I'm old?

MIRANDA

You're not in love with me. You're in love with yourself, and in *lust* with me. But don't worry, the way you make me feel, not only will I make love to you when you're old, I'll do you while you're dying. Hell, I'll do you after you're dead

STEVEN

Ummm., coming while I'm going, I like that

MIRANDA

Yeah, you'll be a stiff with a stiff. Just enjoy being out of control for a little while, Steven. I'm not a threat to your marriage. Only *you* are.

STEVEN

Very funny.
(winces)
I got too much sun today. My private parts are beginning to peel.

MIRANDA
(seductively)

Perhaps If I rub some oil on them...

They move closer together, sink beneath CAMERA horizon.

CUT TO:

EXT. DAY

The Jaguar squeals to a halt on Wilshire Blvd., in front of a large office building.

POV FROM INSIDE CAR

Mike opens the door and slides in next to Leslie. She pulls into traffic.

INTERCUT

                            MIKE
                        (concerned)
        You look awful...beautiful, but awful...what's...

She hands him the note. He reads it, looks up:

                            MIKE
        When did you...?

                            LESLIE
                      (cutting him off)
        An hour ago. His cell phone doesn't answer. What are we
        going to do?

                            MIKE
        What do you mean what are we going to do? It's a hoax. It has
        to be! What time is he due to land?

                            LESLIE
                      (checks car clock)
        About eleven hours from now.

Mike picks up car phone, punches 411.

MIKE

Air India flight information, please.

He listens, disconnects, punches in the number, waits:

MIKE

I'd like to check on a passenger on your flight ...
(to Leslie)
What was it?

LESLIE

Shit, I don't know. We'll have to call back. Hang up and call Dianne.

He punches in another number.

MIKE

Dianne...Mike Emerson...what flight was Steven on? No, nothing's wrong.

LESLIE

Ask her if ...

MIKE

She says there's no way he can be reached until it lands.

Leslie grimaces, taps the wheel.

MIKE

I'll call you back. We're in Leslie's car if you need either of us.

He dials again, waits....

                    MIKE
          Yes, your flight 0011...can I find out if a certain passenger is on
          board?

Leslie meanwhile, has pulled into a side street and parked, leaving the engine running.

                    MIKE
          Steven Green...Lagos...that's OK, I'll hold on.

Nervously, they wait.

                    MIKE
          Yes, I know he was listed...you can't, huh? OK, I'll call you
          back. (hangs up)
          They think he was on the plane, but there's no way to know for
          sure until it lands.

                    LESLIE
                    (weary)
          What now?

                    MIKE
          Let's keep it to ourselves for the moment. Look, Leslie,
          Steven's a sweetheart, not an enemy in the world. It can't be
          true.

                    LESLIE
                    (can't hold it in any longer, begins to cry)
          I know, Mike...who could wish him harm?

She puts her head down on the wheel, body trembling with fear.

INSERT

Mike puts his consoling hand on her knee.

DISSOLVE - The sun has gone down on Tetoni Ladas Island - it's getting dark.

MED. - STEVEN AND MIRANDA ON THE BEACH

Covered in banana leaves, sleep tightly wound around each other. A moment...they stir, eyes open, they nuzzle and kiss. Then, somewhere under the leaves, there is movement – Miranda's head slowly disappears beneath the leaves.

ON STEVEN

He stretches mightily, a beatific smile covers his face.

CUT TO:

EXT. GREEN MANSION - NIGHT

INT. LIVING ROOM

Mike, asleep, jacket and tie off is curled up in a fetal position on the couch.

ANGLE ON

Leslie, in a bathrobe pads barefoot into the room with a tray of coffee. She looks like hell. Putting the tray on the coffee table, she shakes Mike awake.

INTERCUT

        MIKE
        (startled)
 Huh ...

        LESLIE
 Please wake up, Mike..

He sits up, rubs where his body aches. He yawns, stretches. licks his lips.

                    MIKE
                　(reacts)
Ugh, tastes like a tribe of pygmies camped overnight in my mouth.
            (reaches for a coffee cup)

                    LESLIE
I wish I could laugh. What do we do now? He wasn't on the plane, didn't check into his hotel, he didn't show up at the safari office, and he hasn't called.

                    MIKE
Look, Leslie, I agree we should start worrying, but I'm against going to the police. Steven is well known - this could hit the reality shows.

                    LESLIE
            (wondering what Steven sees in him)
Mike, would you mind getting the papers.

ANGLE

He gets up, trudges to the front door, opens it, reaches down for the LA, NY Times, and Wall Street Journal, starts to turn back into house, spots something on the lawn that arouses his curiosity.

FOLLOW HIM:

Stepping down into the path, gingerly avoiding little gifts from the neighborhood dogs, goes to a soggy brown paper-wrapped package tied in string.

INSERT:

He picks it up, examining it.

BACK ON HIM

Returning through front door and into living room.

INT. LIVING ROOM -SAME

                MIKE
I found this on the lawn. The sprinklers got it.

                LESLIE
Oh, God, Mike…

                MIKE
Leslie, would you please stop saying that..
            (hands her the package)

She starts tearing it open.

                MIKE
Hold on… don't panic…let's be careful. It could be evidence.

Cautiously, she opens it, careful not to destroy any of the wrappings.

INSERT

Revealing a corner of the contents;

ON HER FACE

She lets out a gasp and thrusts the package at Mike.

                LESLIE
            (anguished)
They've got him… I'll never see Steven again.

                MIKE
            (reaches for package)
Here, let me see that…

He opens it, extracts a pair of pajamas.

ANGLE

A note falls out. He reaches down and picks it up, reads;

ON HIS FACE

Grim. He hands the note to Leslie.

ON MIKE

As she reads, Mike holds out the pajama top. Is that a BLOODSTAIN just below the initials SG?

ON HER - She looks up at him.

INTERCUT:

                      LESLIE
How am I going to do this? We don't have twenty million dollars?

                      MIKE
In 24 hours yet. I think we have to call the police.

                      LESLIE
                    (flares)
You're crazy. It says they'll make sausages out of him and feed it our dog. He's my husband. I don't care about the money. I want him back!

                      MIKE
Take it easy, Leslie, we'll figure out a way.
                    (thinks a moment)
What else is there of value besides this house, the one at the beach and the condo in Vail?

                    LESLIE
          The cars, the boat...my jewelry. The business, of course.

                    MIKE
          The business isn't disposable overnight. I told him a thousand
          times to go public...we could have sold shares. We'll just have
          to dump everything else.

                    LESLIE
               (fighting panic)
          Fine. They want the money tomorrow. Mike, we've got to get
          him back.

                    MIKE
               (soothing)
          We will, Leslie, we will. Don't worry.

He puts his arm around her. She sinks into him, sobbing quietly.

INSERT

Almost imperceptibly, his arm drops ever so slowly, until his hand is resting on her ass

CUT TO:

EXT. DAY

The SUN rises over Tetoni Ladas island. Another beautiful day in paradise.

Steven, red as a beet, has fashioned a kind of loincloth over his groin and is fishing with his bare hands in rock pools along the shore, desperately trying to snag some protein. So far, no luck.

WIDE:

Miranda, whose nakedness becomes more fetching the more we see of her, is picking mangoes off a tree behind the beach. They never had it so good in "Blue Lagoon". As they meet in mid-beach and embrace;

>	STEVEN
> I want you to be available to me when we get back. You can work if
> you want to, but I'm opening up a bank account for you.
> 		(a leer)
> And I'm planning on making regular deposits.
>
> 	MIRANDA
> Mmm…sounds good, but just remember that there's a severe penalty for early withdrawal.

REVERSE SHOT:

Steven's loincloth beginning to slip, falls to the beach.

CUT TO:

INT. WEST L.A.P.D., Detective Division.

Leslie and Mike being interviewed by three DETECTIVES.

The YOUNG MAN in charge wears a terrible toupee, looks like he cut it out of a corner of the industrial carpeting covering the floor.

OTHER MAN is older, overweight, bordering on obese. He wears suspenders, to which he's pinned his badge.

The third, a WOMAN, is black and stylishly dressed. Although short and slender, you wouldn't want to mess with her.

A FEMALE CADET, bearing a tray with six coffees in styrofoam cups joins them.

> YOUNG DETECTIVE (SCHWARTZ)
> (heated)

So why are you here? You don't need us if you just want to pay them off!

> LESLIE
> (stands abruptly)

That's what I've been saying all along. C'mon, Mike, let's get out of here, he's right, we don't need them!

> MIKE

Wait a minute, Leslie.
> (pulls her back down to Schwartz)

This is all the money they have in the world, everything they've worked for for fifteen years...they want it back!

> LESLIE
> (jumps up again)

Mike, you idiot...they'll get him killed. We made money before...we'll make it again. It's Steven's life we're talking about!

> BLACK WOMAN COP (ITAZUMI)
> (a South African accent)

Mrs. Green, may I say something here?

Leslie looks at her, struck by Itazumi's quiet, but commanding voice.

> LESLIE

Yes, of course, officer...

> ITAZUMI
> (holding the kidnap notes)

I'm Detective Mafolo Itazumi. I'm married too, and I love my husband. And in your place, I'd probably want to do the same. But I'm a cop, and I see it differently.

Leslie, impressed sits down.

INTERCUT

                    ITAZUMI

You fly often?

                    LESLIE

Yes.

                    ITAZUMI

If an engine quit, would you go into the cockpit and take over from the pilot?

                    LESLIE

No ....

                    ITAZUMI

And if Steven needed heart surgery...

                    LESLIE

Look, I see where you're going, but...

                    ITAZUMI

We're professionals, Mrs. Green. We do this for a living. We're much more successful than TV shows give us credit for. And we have a plan...

Leslie's listening now.

ON ITAZUMI - Looks at Schwartz, gets a nod.

                    ITAZUMI

Nobody's sure he's been kidnapped. Husbands run away all the time. However, in this case, it doesn't look too likely. He has too much good stuff, and no problems - that we know about...

With Leslie's approval, she continues;

                    ITAZUMI
Get the money together. We'll get your husband back. And whoever's got him. Plus the money.

ON LESLIE

Somehow, she trusts this woman's quiet assurance; she looks at Mike, then at the others, then Itazumi.

                    LESLIE
What's the plan?

                    ITAZUMI
I have to go to the ladies room, don't you?

TRAVEL WITH THEM

As she takes Leslie's arm to guide her, she looks back at the three men, and says over her shoulder:

                    ITAZUMI
Drives them crazy ... just what is it we do in there?

CUT TO:

INT. Jaguar, on SANTA MONICA BLVD., heading EAST towards BEVERLY HILLS

                    LESLIE
I'm so torn, Mike... I believe her, but...

                    MIKE
What's the set up?

                    LESLIE
We make the payoff, they follow. Helicopter, no lights. Decoy cars at lover's lanes and at both ends. We hope for the best.

                    MIKE
Hell, Leslie, that's no different from any TV show. I'm glad you changed your mind, but why?

                    LESLIE
It's the two notes, the way Itazumi read them. They're amateurs, and they're scared. She said we'd make the payoff, and they'd kill him. This way we have a chance.

ON LESLIE

Her mind is made up. She's grim, and as she drives, tears roll down her cheeks.

CUT TO:

EXT. TETONI LADAS ISLAND - DAY

High noon. It's hot.

ANGLE ON Steven, stretched out under a coconut tree, exhausted by sunburn the heat, lack of proper nutrition, but most of all by Miranda, who, humming, has shinnied up a banana tree, her bare behind right now her most prominent feature.

M.C.U. ON HER

As she pulls off bananas, throwing them in Steven's direction.

C.U. ON HIM – As one hits him in the stomach, shocking him awake;

                    STEVEN
         Ooofff!! Miranda ... dammit!

BACK ON HER

Giggling, she slides down the trunk. 36 hours ago, the sight of all that luscious naked flesh in positions we usually don't see in city life would have made him a hard act to follow. Right now, however, after all the action he's had, he's beginning to dread her coming any closer.

HIS POV

But closer she comes:

> MIRANDA
> (cooing)
> Steven, darling ....

CU: His face - A sickly smile;

> STEVEN
> Listen, baby, not right now... please?

> MIRANDA
> I must, because it's obvious that you, sir, are suffering from *DSB*.

> STEVEN
> *DSB*? What's *DSB*?

> MIRANDA
> Why, Deadly Sperm Backup, and Nurse Miranda has the cure.

ON HER - More relentless than Terminator One, she advances. He groans, but to no avail, as he disappears beneath her body.

CUT TO:

INT. EXECUTIVE OFFICES, FIRST BANK OF BEVERLY HILLS - DAY

Leslie, Mike and MAX HOROWITZ, owner and president of the bank, huddle in Max's opulently appointed office.

Max is a tiny, totally bald man with large, black-rimmed eyeglasses, behind which his eyes seem huge.

INTERCUT

                    MAX

It's been done before, of course. But it was for Frank Sinatra. His son had been kidnapped, and they opened the vault for him. But it was only for a quarter million. (he stops a moment to reminisce) Back then a lot of money.

                    LESLIE

Max, you bankrolled us. You watched us grow from nothing. We did a hundred million last year.

                    MAX

In sales, Leslie, sales. Not net.

                    MIKE
                (exasperated)

I don't like this, Max. Are you gonna' help us, or not? You've made a lot of money with Steven and Leslie.

                    MAX

Yes, yes, of course, but no bank has that kind of cash on hand, only the Federal Reserve. Do you know anyone there? I don't!

                    LESLIE
                (towers over Max)

I swear, Max, when Steven comes home, he's gonna' beat the shit out of you and if he doesn't, I will!

MIKE
(restrains Leslie)
Cool it, Leslie.
(turns to Max)
Max, what can you really do?

MAX
Well, you've got five million eight equity in the Bel-Air house, three million two in Malibu. And the condo, which you bought for cash, I'll personally buy for the assessed value of a million five. I think I may be able to find a buyer for the houses, but if not, the bank will take them over, and we'll hold them until you can buy back the notes.

MIKE
That's only 10 million. What about the cars and the boat?

MAX
You'll have to get rid of the cars yourself. The boat, I wouldn't know what to do with.

LESLIE
What about my jewelry? It's worth half a million at least.

MIKE
We'll have to dump everything for the value of the gold and stones.

LESLIE
Max, how much will you lend us on the business?

MAX
The business, Leslie, is Steven.
(reacts to her murderous look)
And you, of course! He's been brilliant in research and bringing out new products, but it's held down your growth. I can't give you anything on it.

                    (thinks a minute)
            Perhaps when your new line with the elephant stuff...

                         LESLIE
                        (enraged)
            Get me outta' here, Mike, before I kill the little bastard!

                         MIKE
                        (to Max)
            Draw up those papers now, Max. Fax them to Leslie's house.
            I'll see she signs them and get them back to you. And
            remember, we need cash by tomorrow!

ON MAX

He gulps, nods and is glad to see them out of there. He does, however, allow himself a small smile as he closes the door.

CUT TO:

TETONI LADAS ISLAND – VERY EARLY MORNING

CAMERA finds Miranda, sleeping in their little handmade bower, cuddled in fetus position – looking like an angel. Camera PULLS BACK and UP over the trees to locate Steven scooping fresh rain water from an indentation in a rock - gulping down the last three of his little blue pills.

CUT TO:

VAN NUYS BLVD. - DAY

North of the freeway. Miles of used car lots. A procession: Steven's Rolls convertible, the Green Jaguar and the red Ferrari Testarossa travel slowly.

ANGLE FROM ACROSS THE STREET

The Rolls pulls alongside a car lot and stops, others pull in behind.

Leslie emerges from the Rolls, slams the door and walks into the lot. Esmeralda, the maid, is behind the wheel of the Jaguar. Mike, driving the Ferrari, exits and motioning to Esmeralda to stay put, follows Leslie.

CUT TO:

USED CAR LOT

"THE SIAMESE TWINS" - dominated by a huge Buddhist temple set painted red, gold and white.

Leslie and Mike, exasperated, haggling, and gesturing towards the street with TWO smiling SIAMESE (THAI) MEN who look exactly alike but mercifully are not joined at the hip, or anywhere else. They wear orange sarongs and have shaved heads. One has a copy of the Kelly Blue Book in his hand, and no matter how pissed off and upset Leslie and Mike are, the Siamese men never let go of their smiles.

POV FROM SIDEWALK

They stalk off, enter the cars and drive away.

CUT TO:

ANOTHER USED CAR LOT - SAME

"THE CARAVAN" - Balloons and tents. A CAMEL, two humps, is tethered in the driveway.

KIDS gawk. THREE excited MIDDLE EASTERN TYPES are jabbering to themselves in some language, while Leslie and Mike cast exasperated looks at each other. They throw up their hands and leave.

CUT TO:

EXT. STILL ANOTHER USED CAR LOT - SAME

MASAI MOTORS - A Hollywood representation of an African village. Grass huts house tall, thin, dark salesmen wearing elaborate hairdressing and brightly colored robes. Several goats and a few cows wander between the rows of cars.

Standing at the dirt path entrance, Leslie and Mike look at each other, shake their heads "no", and beeline for their cars.

EXT. Later that afternoon.

They are way out at the end of the valley, all the store signs are in SPANISH. The caravan pulls into a gas station and over to the pumps. Tiredly, they emerge from their cars.

                      ESMERALDA
Meesis ... my family live here. My uncle, Antonio, he in car business. Maybe he help.

                      LESLIE
              (looks at her, shakes her head)
Esmeralda, you're a treasure ... but we need a lot of money, and we need it fast.

                      ESMERALDA
Si, meesis ... I call.

She goes to a pay phone.

ANGLE ON ESMERALDA - In Spanish, we hear that Uncle Antonio will be pleased to see them.

ON LESLIE AND MIKE

Look at each other and shrug ... what the hell!

CUT TO: EXT. SAME

Some minutes later, the caravan ascends a long, dusty dirt road, entering a compound of several houses surrounded by a barbed wire fence, in the foothills above the valley floor. UNCLE ANTONIO, an Anthony Quinn lookalike, strides out to greet them, followed by at least SEVEN OTHER FAMILY MEMBERS and as many barking dogs.

CUT TO: INT.

They are ushered into ANTONIO'S HOUSE, cool and dark. The beers all around hit their spots

> ANTONIO
> (very courtly)
> A great pleasure, madam ... Esmeralda has told us so much....

> LESLIE
> Thank you, Antonio. I can't go into it, but we don't have much time.

> ANTONIO
> Si, Si. Tell you what. You have papers with you?

> MIKE
> (a little suspicious)
> Yes, we do, but ...

> ANTONIO
> I have customers for your cars. I give you five hundred thousand cash now. A deal?

Leslie looks at Mike; can this be true?

> LESLIE
> (beginning to get it)
> Look, Antonio, we also have a boat in the Marina. A Cigarette, with 400 horses.

ANTONIO
(eyes light up)
You have papers with you?

LESLIE
Yes..yes.

ANTONIO
I give you another three hundred fifty thousand.

LESLIE
OK, Antonio.
(to Mike)
The papers, and the boat keys.

Mike, skeptical, digs in the envelope he's brought. Antonio goes to a steel box on the coffee table, brings it to them, opens it.

INSERT - It's stuffed with cash.

BACK ON ANTONIO

He counts out $850,000.

ON LESLIE

She signs the transfer papers and they're out the door, when they realize, no wheels.

ANTONIO
(gets it)
A small gift.

(to Rafelito)
Rafelito, give them the keys to your car.

RAFELITO, one of Esmeralda's seven brothers, fishes in his pocket, tosses set of keys to Leslie.

ANOTHER ANGLE

Antonio walks them over to a purple and black 1975 Chevy Monte Carlo, chopped and channeled, complete with fur dashboard, oversize dice hanging from the rear view mirror and severely darkened windows.

POV

As Leslie, Mike and Esmeralda pile into the Chevy, Rafelito and his brothers are already at work, removing the license plates from their new cars.

INSIDE CHEVY

Mike starts the Chevy, a real smoker, and heads for the valley as Leslie and Esmeralda wave out the back window to the retreating Escobar family.

                        MIKE
    I should have brought my shirts. They could have laundered
    those too!

                        LESLIE
                  (smiles slyly)
    Why, Michael, whatever could you mean? They're obviously
    just a hard working immigrant family, taking advantage of our
    capitalist system... just like we do!

CUT TO:

EXT. BEL AIR - THE GREEN MANSION - SUNSET

The Monte Carlo parked in the driveway.

CUT TO:

INT. DEN - SAME

ON MIKE

Ripping papers from the fax, reading them quickly, handing them to Leslie for signature.

Front door bell RINGS.

ANGLE ON

Esmeralda answers it.

O.S. CONVERSATION - THEN FOOTSTEPS

ANGLE INTO THE DEN

Max enters with an older JAPANESE COUPLE and a YOUNGER JAPANESE MAN acting as interpreter.

AN UNEASY INTRODUCTION

FOLLOW LESLIE - as she takes them on a tour.

BACK TO MIKE - faxing signed copies back to the bank while bundling originals for Max.

DISSOLVE TO:

EXT: TETONI LADAS ISLAND - Almost dark

It's been raining most of the day.

ON STEVEN AND MIRANDA

Putting final touches on a crude platform they've built on two low tree limbs that intersect about 10 feet from the ground. They've covered its floor with banana leaves, and have bent branches over, hooking them together to form a shelter.

The remains of their ground fire are soggy, and they are cold.

C.U: AS THEY HUDDLE TOGETHER

Wearing all the clothes they have. Steven is miserable, wishing he had never come.

THROUGH THE TREES

They fall asleep sitting up and leaning on one another. The rain drips in.

Suddenly, Steven SITS UP, grabs his stomach with a pained, bewildered look – makes a quick decision.

ON STEVEN – as he makes a mad dash through the underbrush. Stumbling over rocks until he's out of sight – and hearing of Miranda, he whips off his loincloth and squats in a near-perfect imitation of his poodle, Rush Limbaugh, several days ago in his kitchen.

ON STEVEN'S FACE – contorted in agony and then relief. A loud groan escapes his lips. He looks around;

                        STEVEN
          Oh, no…what am I gonna' use for….

No leaves handy, he scoops up a handful of wet sand and…..

                        STEVEN
                        (con't.)
    Owww…….

ON MIRANDA – she hears the groan, the cry of pain, smiles, and goes back to sleep.

DISSOLVE:

EXT. THE GREEN MANSION - LATER SAME EVENING

Lights ablaze. At the front door, the Japanese Couple and their Interpreter bow formally to Leslie and Mike, who bow in return. They enter Max's CAR and drive away.

ON LESLIE AND MIKE - face each other and bow deeply.

POV from across the street;

A dark-colored, four-door sedan parked out of the light. CAMERA travels in revealing the driver, Itazumi, taking in the scene.

CUT TO:

TETONI LADAS ISLAND - EXT. NIGHT

Black as pitch.

SOUNDS tell us we're near the ocean; bushes rustle in the wind, crickets mating. A new sound, something straining, giving way.

Suddenly, a loud CRACK, and a resounding CRASH.

From Steven and Miranda's anguished voices, we know their little tree house is on the cold, wet ground, and so are they.

CUT TO:

EXT. DOWNTOWN L.A.- THE JEWELRY DISTRICT - EARLY MORNING

HASIDIC MEN with sample cases and COURIERS scurry in and out of the Spring Street building housing the JEWELRY MART.

Leslie, heavily dressed for the season, and Mike enter, cross the lobby, peer at the directory, look at each other, shrug and head for the elevator, which swallows them.

INT. Elevator doors open. They emerge and start down corridor, stopping at a likely door, push the buzzer and are admitted.

CUT TO:

INT. DIAMOND CUTTER'S OFFICE

Behind the cramped counter, a large HASID MAN in black pants, white shirt, sleeves puffed up and held with garters, full beard, side locks and yarmulke.

> DIAMOND CUTTER
> (YONKEL)
> Nu?

Leslie and Mike exchange looks; definitely a new world for them.

> LESLIE
> Ahh, I have some jewelry to sell?

> YONKEL
> So, let's see?

Encouraged, Leslie removes her gloves, pulls up her jacket sleeves, revealing a mass of diamond studded tennis bracelets, I.D. bracelets, bracelets with gemstones. Her fingers are covered in rings.

Opening her jacket, we see several diamond and gold necklaces and pendants.

ANGLE ON MIKE

Pushes up his sleeves; he's wearing half-a-dozen Rolexes, obviously Steven's.

> YONKEL
> (impressed, whistles softly)
> You have papers?

> LESLIE
> (to Mike)
> What is this with everyone wanting papers? Do you think they all know each other? (to Yonkel) Yes, insurance appraisals. Will that do?

> YONKEL
> (nods)
> For me, it's too big. I need help.

He goes to the telephone, dials, and in YIDDISH, we surmise he is inviting his fellow dealers to join him in a look.

CUT TO:

The little office is jammed with HASIDS, big, small, short, fat, all dressed similarly. One even wears a long black coat and a pie shaped fur hat. Several have jeweler's loupes to their eyes, examining the merchandise.

INTERCUT:

Everyone is sweating and haggling. The noise level is awesome.

CUT TO:

Tiny BATHROOM of Yonkel's office.

ON LESLIE - Stuffing greenbacks into her bra, into her pantyhose, front and back, smoothing her clothes over.

CUT TO:

EXT. JEWELRY MART

Leslie and Mike exit. She's near exhaustion. Between Yonkel and his friends, Uncle Antonio, and Mr. and Mrs. Hashimoto, she is a long way from her serene Bel-Air lifestyle of just three days ago.

                    LESLIE
          Whew, what a day, and it's not even 10 o'clock yet
                    (looks at her watch)
          We have fourteen hours to make the payoff.
                    (pats her new, voluptuous figure)
          We're 400 grand closer, where are we now?

                    MIKE
          With Hashimoto's money today, we've got eleven seven-fifty
          cash. We'll never do it. We've got to think of something.

                    LESLIE
          I've got an idea. We'll be mortgaging the company for years,
          but it might be the only way.

                    MIKE
          What?
                    LESLIE
                    (getting excited)
          The distributors across the country, and the buyers. If we can
          cut the right deal, give them deeply discounted future delivery
          contracts, we can probably get cash advances by wire.

                    MIKE
                    (catching her enthusiasm)
          It might work...Let's get to a phone.

                    LESLIE
          We'll be broke forever ... but it doesn't matter.

As they head towards the parking garage;

POV - Det. Itazumi emerges from a storefront. She watches them walk away.

CUT TO:

INT. ELEVATOR

Itazumi hums as she watches floor numbers flash by, stop at 53. Doors open to executive floor of ARIADNE Cosmetics.

REVERSE

She strides out and over to receptionist, a BEAUTIFUL YOUNG GIRL.

INSERT: Wall clock reminds us it's 10 o'clock.

> ITAZUMI
> (flashes her ID/badge case)
> Good morning, Detective Itazumi, LAPD. I'd like to talk to Mr. Green's secretary, please.

> RECEPTIONIST
> Certainly, one moment please.
> (dials switchboard telephone)
> Dianne? There's a Detective Itazumi here to see you ... thank you.
> (to Itazumi)
> Go through the double doors, turn to your right, down the corridor. Mr. Green's office will be on your left.

> ITAZUMI
> Thanks.

As she heads towards the doors, several WOMEN executives, assistants, secretaries, etc., carrying reports, files, converge with her. All of them are particularly beautiful.

Itazumi reaches and enters Steven's compound. Dianne stands to greet her.

INTERCUT

> DIANNE
> (a little surprised it's a woman)
> Detective Itazumi? I'm Dianne Hardwick.

ITAZUMI
Nice to meet you.

DIANNE
(uncertain how to act, offers a chair and a smile)
Now what did I do?

ITAZUMI
Nothing, I hope. Just a few questions about your boss, if you don't mind

DIANNE
Whew. No, I don't mind.

ITAZUMI
How long have you worked here?

DIANNE
Eleven years, altogether.

ITAZUMI
Always for Mr. Green?

DIANNE
No, I started in the art department as a trainee, right out of Art Center in Pasadena. It was my first job. The company had just started.

ITAZUMI
You said altogether, what did you mean?

DIANNE
I left after six years to join an ad agency, but the advertising business on the West coast failed. I needed a job and Steven took me back.

ITAZUMI
So you've been here this time, what?

DIANNE
The last five.

ITAZUMI
Anyone ever tell you look a lot like Mrs. Green?

DIANNE
(sips her coffee)
Yeah... I've heard that.

ITAZUMI
I notice a lot of pretty women work here.

DIANNE
It's almost a condition of employment.

ITAZUMI
(smiles)
Mr. Green set that policy?

DIANNE
Steven personally hires the women here.

ITAZUMI
Uh, huh... Any of the other women call him Steven?

DIANNE
Yes, all of them.

ITAZUMI
Mr. Green have any enemies, do you think?

DIANNE
(eyes narrow)
Enemies, how do you mean?

ITAZUMI
He ever hurt anyone, disappoint anyone….screw anyone?

DIANNE
I never met a detective before. You always choose your words so carefully?

ITAZUMI
You mean screw?

Dianne says nothing.

ITAZUMI.
Are you aware, Miss Hardwick, your boss may be missing?

DIANNE
I know he's not in Africa ... and that his wife is worried.

ITAZUMI
Are you worried?

DIANNE
You mean for my job? I'd hate to be unemployed in this economy.

ITAZUMI
I have the feeling you're not his biggest fan.

DIANNE
It's not easy being close to him.
(her eyes begin to tear)

ITAZUMI
Why not?

DIANNE
He's the kind of guy who promises a lot, but doesn't deliver. You know - you're a woman.

ITAZUMI
You were pretty close once, huh?

DIANNE
You could say that. I was young.

ITAZUMI
This job must pay well.

DIANNE
(blows her nose)
It does, actually ... most of the time, it's OK.

ITAZUMI
Except when he's being close to some of the other women around here?

DIANNE
(hits the nerve)
Yeah..here..and there.

ITAZUMI
So, you handle his personal life too?

DIANNE
You mean his hotel rooms..dinners..his little trips?
(flash of anger)
It's pathetic the way he treats us..he thinks every woman loves him.

                    ITAZUMI
               Like you still do?

No answer.

                    ITAZUMI
               Last question, Dianne, and I'll leave you alone. Can you think
               of anyone who would want to hurt Steven?

                    DIANNE
               Yeah...a lot of people. Just look around you.

Itazumi nods, stands up and leaves Steven's office.

ANGLE ON

Itazumi approaching the elevator, punches the button, begins to hum again...looks around...lots of pretty WOMEN moving about. Elevator arrives, she steps in, doors close.

ANOTHER ANGLE - ELEVATOR BANK

As doors close on Itazumi, another elevator arrives; doors open discharging Leslie and Mike, who nod to receptionist and disappear through office double doors.

CUT TO:

Leslie and Mike entering Leslie's office. Logo on door says that Leslie is president.

                    LESLIE
               Mike, get on the computer and start drafting a sample contract.
                         (calls out to secretary)
               Pam....get me a list of our distributors worldwide, and our
               major buyers, department stores, catalogs, everything you can
               lay your hands on.

CUT TO:

PAM and other assistants; a flurry of activity.

CUT TO: TETONI LADAS ISLAND - DAY THREE

Steven and Miranda are "packed", and Steven is more than ready to leave. Although sunburned, he looks tired, exhausted - his safari clothes are dirty, faded and ragged. Miranda's sundress, naked as she mostly was, looks new. She is tanned, and fresh as a daisy.

They wait under the shade of a coconut tree, scanning the horizon for the seaplane. They don't have a lot to say to each other.

Suddenly, a WHOOSHING sound and a loud THUD. Steven jumps as a five-pound coconut hits the ground at 50 mph right next to him. A few inches to the left and he would have been a dead man.

ON HIS REACTION

CUT TO:

AN APARTMENT BUILDING IN BEVERLY HILLS - DAY

Itazumi parks her unmarked sedan in front, exits and approaches building, peers at tenant register, enters.

Itazumi in front of an apartment door, which opens, revealing DOTTIE GREEN, a small, elderly woman, mid- 70s, bleached blonde, heavy make up, long, pampered fingernails. Where is Ruth Gordon now that we need her'?

>   DOTTIE
> Another witness from Jehovah? Listen, God is my co-pilot, but only on Friday nights.

>   ITAZUMI
> Mrs. Green, I'm a police officer.
>   (holds up ID).

                    DOTTIE
I know the Mayor ... He told me I could park overnight in front of my house. I have asthma.

                    ITAZUMI
Whoa, Mrs. Green. I want to talk to you about your son.

                    DOTTIE
I used to have a son. My son he's not anymore.

                    ITAZUMI
May I come in?

                    DOTTIE
OK, you'll have something to eat ... we'll talk about it.

Itazumi enters and sits on the living room couch, while Dottie goes to boil some water.

INSERT

Lots of framed photos around of Steven as a baby, child, young adult, adult, wedding pictures, etc. There is just one picture of a man who probably was Dottie's husband and Steven's father.

ANGLE ON

Dottie enters with tea in glasses, Ritz crackers and strawberry jam, sets them down and sits opposite Itazumi.

                    DOTTIE
So?

Itazumi stirs sugar into her tea, looks up at Dottie;

ITAZUMI
What do you think happened to your son?

DOTTIE
He went off the beam when he married that woman. He knows I'm right all these years and he's run away. He's afraid to face me.

ITAZUMI
Steven is 40 years old, Mrs. Green. Do you really think he's run away?

DOTTIE
He's done it before. He ran away when he was fifteen, threw his schoolbooks down the sewer and took a bus to Florida to follow some tramp. I got him back. I called every police department in every state. They found him and they brought him back to me.

ITAZUMI
How are you going to get him back this time?

DOTTIE
This time the big shot is on his own. His father's insurance money I lent him to start his business. That woman he made his partner, not me.

ITAZUMI
So you feel left out?

DOTTIE
Women come and go, but only his mother will be there to save him in the end.

ITAZUMI
What if he doesn't come back? What if he's being held against his will?

                    DOTTIE
          It wouldn't hurt him to learn a little humility.

Itazumi looks thoughtful, stands.

                    ITAZUMI
          Thank you for the tea, Mrs. Green.

                    DOTTIE
          Do you have children, officer?

                    ITAZUMI
          Not yet, why?

                    DOTTIE
          Because they're a pain in the ass forever, that's why. I don't
          recommend it.

Itazumi smiles, heads for the door, exits.

CUT TO:

EXT. NIGHT - BLUE HEAVEN

A cop hangout on a side street somewhere off SANTA MONICA BLVD., in WEST LA, near the police station on Purdue Avenue.

CUT TO: INT.

Loud, smoky, inhabited by cops, most off duty, some still on.

CAMERA finds Itazumi and Lt. Schwartz at a corner table in the back. Schwartz has built a pyramid of .38 special shells and is gingerly attempting to place just one more on the top.

INTERCUT

> ITAZUMI
> If he was kidnapped, there's a hell of a lot of suspects. His own mother hates him.
> (she sips her beer).

> SCHWARTZ
> So what...my mother hates me too. Comes with being a Jewish boy. What else you got?

> ITAZUMI
> His secretary was once his girlfriend. He dumped her and now part of her job is setting up his other affairs.

> SCHWARTZ
> Must pay well

> ITAZUMI
> That's what I said... she still loves him.

> SCHWARTZ
> What about the lawyer? He's supposed to be Green's best friend.

> ITAZUMI
> From what I've seen, looks like he wants to be the wife's best friend too.

Schwartz's pyramid collapses, bullets falling to the table and rolling off on the floor. He dives down to round them up.

> SCHWARTZ
> Shit....

As he comes up, he bumps his head on the table corner, knocking his toupee slightly astray. Itazumi tries hard not to notice.

> SCHWARTZ (con't.)
> (trying to be cool)
> What about that cute wife?

> ITAZUMI
> You know, before I was a cop, when I was teaching 8th grade at St. Vivian's, Sister Cornelius would sometimes take over my Latin class. She always asked the kids "Qui Bono?"...who benefits? It's a good life lesson. (pause)
> I don't see how she benefits. If he was snatched, she loses everything. If he's just off with some bimbette, half is hers anyway.

> SCHWARTZ
> (stands up)
> So just about everyone he knows, except his wife, is a suspect. *There's* a switch. I gotta pee. In six hours the payoff gets made. We'll see what's what.

He makes his way to the men's room, surreptitiously adjusting his hairpiece.

CUT TO:

VAULT ROOM - FIRST BEVERLY HILLS BANK

Max, Leslie and Mike at a table, surrounded by stacks of money, wearing rubber thumbs counting greenbacks, and mumbling figures.

> MAX
> Nine hundred ten thousand…nine hundred eleven thousand...

> LESLIE
> A hundred ten thousand, a hundred twenty thousand...

                    MIKE
            (stuffing stacks in a large brown case)
    Two million six even...
                    (stops to write down figures on a pad.)
    Lots more to go.

Leslie glances at her watch.

                    LESLIE
    Faster, guys ... we have to be at the checkpoint in 2 hours.

DISSOLVE

EXT. NIGHT

FIREHOUSE at intersection of Mulholland and Beverly Glen, all lit up.

INT: BATTALION CHIEF'S OFFICE

Arranged around a table covered with maps are Leslie, Mike, Lt. Schwartz, Itazumi, Fat Detective from the interview, assorted OTHER POLICE and FIRE OFFICERS, including a jump-suited HELICOPTER PILOT.

INSERT: WALL CLOCK reads 10:30.

                    SCHWARTZ
    Are we in sync here?

                    LESLIE
            (consults kidnap note)
    Yes, yes. We drive Mulholland west from Topanga. According to the note, past the hairpin turn, 6.3 miles from where we start, there'll be a queen of hearts playing card tacked on a tree on the valley side. I'm to drive exactly nine more minutes, throw the suitcase over the edge and keep going.

                    ITAZUMI
    We'll be covering you... spy in the sky, a Lo-Jack on your car, and you're wired. You'll be in our sights all the way.

SCHWARTZ
Both ends of Mulholland will be surveilled. Keep in mind, it's critical to remember exactly where that playing card is... it's our only marker.

MIKE
We will...God, I'm nervous...anybody got a cigarette?

Assorted cops reach in their pockets.

LESLIE
(scorn in her voice)
A cigarette? You don't smoke! This is not some TV show. Get a grip! Maybe I should do this myself.

Mike sheepishly waves away the opened packs offered him.

SCHWARTZ
OK, let's go.

They troop outside. Helicopter pilot gets into unmarked car for ride to VAN NUYS airport, others move into their vehicles.

Leslie, Mike, Schwartz and Itazumi walk to Monte Carlo.

SCHWARTZ
(shakes his head)
How the mighty have fallen.
(to Mike)
What about your car, barrister? This cholomobile might not even make it.

MIKE
(defensive)
I have a cherry '57 Porsche speedster...gimme a break.

                    LESLIE
                    (a sneer)
      My lawyer, the pussy.
                    (to Schwartz)
      This car will do fine. I'm certain it's fed a lot of dust to your
      squad cars, Lieutenant.

She goes to trunk, opens it. Mike lifts out large brown case with the money. They get in. Leslie's the driver.

                    SCHWARTZ
                    (looks at his watch)
      Chopper is airborne and flying dark at 23:50 ... that's 11:50 to
      you. Over the site at midnight. You'll be making the payoff at
      approximately the same time. OK, g'wan ... we'll see you later.

                    ITAZUM
                    (leans in car, to Leslie)
      Good luck... don't worry, and be strong.

ANGLE INTO MONTE CARLO

Leslie (a bit teary), starts the car, wheels it around, facing out.

CUT TO: EXT. NIGHT

An airfield, somewhere deep in the interior of Mexico. A tin-roofed shack with a windsock and a Coca-Cola sign in the window. A couple of old airliners and crop dusters in various stages of decay are scattered about.

CUT TO: INT. SHACK

Steven, Miranda, and Frankley, disheveled and slightly damp are at a desk. Steven is arguing with ALFONSO, the owner of Aerolineas de Agricultura, S.A., who is also the town's Police Chief, Pharmacist, and disc jockey.

                    STEVEN
Alright, Alfonso, two thousand U.S. dollars, you take us to
Tijuana, we'll get home from there.
          (to Frankley, menacingly)
This is all your our fault!

                    MIRANDA
Steven...grow up! Frankley didn't run out of gas on purpose.
That plane was all he had.

                    STEVEN
If that fishing boat hadn't come along, we would have been
would've been gringoburgers for those sharks.

                    ALFONSO
Si, Senor Estaban, a deal is a deal. I take you almost right now.
Our friend Frankley will fly one of my planes, I fly the other.

                    STEVEN
Oh... I ain't flying with him!

                    MIRANDA
              (to Steven)
I'm very disappointed in you.
              (to Frankley)
I'd be pleased to accompany you, sir. (points at Steven)
And if <u>he</u> doesn't buy you a new airplane, I will!

                    FRANKLEY
              (courtly as ever)
My pleasure, M'am.

Steven glares at both.

> ALFONSO
> (gestures to benches along the wall)
> Make yourselves comfortable, senores and senorita. I will see about petroleo.

They do the best they can arranging themselves along the wall, using Miranda's bag and Frankley's smelly leather jacket for pillows. They could sleep, if it weren't for the cackling chickens searching for insects in the cracked concrete floor just underneath their heads.

DISSOLVE:

NIGHT - INT. MONTE CARLO

Leslie drives, Mike holds suitcase on his lap, their faces lit by dash lights.

> LESLIE
> Hold on, here's where we lose the pavement.

Monte Carlo starts to bump heavily as the road turns from pavement to pot-holed dirt from west of Topanga to the ocean.

POV FROM EXT.

Other than the car's headlights, it is pitch dark.

> MIKE
> Take it easy, Les...

It's a rough ride, as blind curves prevent the headlights from seeing more than 30 feet ahead. Leslie slows;

> MIKE
> (con't.)
> Listen, Les, I'm sorry for what happened back there.

> LESLIE
> I didn't mean what I said either. We're both upset. I just miss him so.
> (her voice breaks)
> We've just got to get him back.

They drive in silence, watching the odometer.

CUT TO: INT. FIREHOUSE

Schwartz and Itazumi monitoring reports from the chopper, from decoy cars with cop couples pretending to be lovers parked at turnouts, and from the radar screen tracking the Lo-Jack device attached to the Monte Carlo.

RADIOS CRACKLE: no contact.

> SCHWARTZ
> Fifteen minutes ... she'll be at the hairpin.

CUT TO: INT. MONTE CARLO

> LESLIE
> Mike...I'm scared.

> MIKE
> Leslie, this is no time... scared of what?

> LESLIE
> The police are gonna' get Steven killed. I can't go through with this.

She brings the Monte Carlo to a shuddering HALT.

FOLLOW HER as she leaps out and goes to the rear, squats under bumper, pulls off Lo-jack and throws it into the bushes.

As she gets back behind the wheel, rips off her wire.

> MIKE
> (babbling)
> Are you crazy, Leslie? Now *we're* in trouble with the cops...that device costs thousands... I'm an officer of the court!

> LESLIE
> (looks at him)
> Mike, we've got to save him ourselves. Are you with me, 'cause if you're not, you can get out here.

> MIKE
> Here?
> (looks out at solid darkness;
> cowardice triumphs)
> He's my best friend. Let's go get him back!

Leslie stamps down on the accelerator, rear wheels spin, and they're off.

CUT TO:

INT. FIREHOUSE - SAME

> SCHWARTZ
> They've stopped ... what the fuck!
> (grabs a microphone.)
> Cholo ... cholo ... what's wrong? ...

Silence.

> SCHWARTZ
> Chopper one ... do you read?

A moment.

> CHOPPER
> (filtered)
> Loud and clear, Lieutenant ... what's up?

SCHWARTZ
Do you have a visual on the cholo?

CHOPPER
(filtered)
Negative ... I think they're turned off their lights.

SCHWARTZ
DAMMIT!

Pounds the table with his fist, causing his toupee to shift slightly.

CUT TO:

EXT. NIGHT - SAME

Monte Carlo running without lights.

Mike hangs out his window, shining a flashlight they brought with them on the road as they slowly navigate, flashing on passing trees, looking for the queen of Hearts.

POV FROM INSIDE THE CAR - THERE IT IS!

Leslie stops the car, jumps out, runs to tree, snatches card off and is behind the wheel again.

ANGLE ON

Leslie, jamming the accelerator as off they go in darkness, with only Mike's flashlight to guide them.

CUT TO: INT. FIREHOUSE - SAME

Schwartz is fuming;

                    SCHWARTZ
          She double-crossed us. I knew *we* should have made the
          payoff...
                    (to Itazumi)
          Only they never would have bought you as the wife.

                    ITAZUMI
          I beg your pardon...wasn't Whoopie married to a white man?

                    SCHWARTZ
                    (resigned)
          Well, *we're* clean. If her husband turns up as Dodger-Dogs,
          she did it!

He picks up microphone:

                    SCHWARTZ (cont)
          Sound retreat ... we're going home.
                    (disgusted)
          C'mon, we'll meet them at the house.

CUT TO:

EXT. NIGHT - SAME

LOCATION SPECIFIED IN KIDNAP NOTE

ANGLE INSIDE CAR

Leslie stops car. Mike gets out with large brown case, goes to valley edge of road, and throws it over the side, gets back in car.

BACK INSIDE

Leslie drives off towards the ocean, still without lights.

CUT TO:

EXT. NIGHT

SOUNDS OF DRONING ENGINES

CAMERA is perched next to the streaming blonde hair of Miranda, seated behind Frankley in the open-air, 2-seater cockpit of an ancient crop duster airplane.

ANGLE FROM ABOVE

They fly low to the ground at 80 mph, directly behind another small plane in which sits Alfonso, with Steven at his rear.

It is pitch dark...only an occasional small cluster of lights below as they pass up the coast of Mexico towards the U.S. border.

VARIOUS C.U.s:

All wear goggles as the wind whips their faces. Miranda, grinning, is thrilled, Steven is terrified, and looks it.

Alfonso probably didn't completely close the valve on the pesticide tank under the wing right beside Steven, and a noxious cloud of chemicals threatens to asphyxiate him.

Suddenly, a LOUD CLATTER startles them, as directly overhead an ominous looking HELICOPTER right out of "Blue Thunder" appears. Clearly lettered on the bottom, the legend "U.S. Border Patrol". Its half-million candlepower searchlight blinds them:

                    VOICE FROM CHOPPER SPEAKER
      This is the United States Border Patrol. You are ordered to
      land immediately. Follow me!

CUT TO:

Chopper zooms ahead, and begins to descend.

ANGLE

In the distance, the lights of the TIJUANA AIRPORT.

FROM ABOVE

Alfonso turns around in his cockpit, shrugs and motions for Frankley to follow him.

CUT TO:

Both crop dusters landing as the chopper hovers.

ANGLE ON

Two carloads of MEXICAN FEDERALES closing in, automatic rifles bristling from their windows.

CUT TO:

EXT. BEL AIR - GREEN MANSION - NIGHT

Parked in the driveway; the Monte Carlo and Itazumi's unmarked police car. Lights blaze from the first floor.

CUT TO: INT. KITCHEN

Leslie calmly serves tea to Itazumi.

SCHWARTZ
(mad as hell. stalks around room)
There must be some way I can have both of you arrested for obstructing justice. (to Itazumi) Make a note. I want to ask the D.A. if I can throw their asses in jail!

Itazumi nods, makes a note. Fat Detective is at a console, manning tape recorder attached to the telephone.

SCHWARTZ
We're staying right here until I figure out what's going on!

LESLIE
Suit yourself, Lieutenant. I did what I thought was right for Steven.
(to Esmeralda)
Pillows and blankets, por favor. (to Schwartz) I'm going to bed. I'm exhausted.

She heads for the stairs.

DISSOLVE TO:

INT. Harshly lit OFFICE COMPLEX somewhere in the Tijuana airport.

Steven, Miranda, Frankley, and Alfonso being interrogated by COL. FERNANDEZ, and his troops:

FERNANDEZ
I'm very puzzled, Mr. Green. We find nothing contraband in the planes or on any of you. But you will agree, this is a very strange vacation, yes?

STEVEN
(scared)
Yes, Colonel, but...

                    FERNANDEZ
    You understand we must now search all of you very carefully,
    yes?
                    (grins at Miranda).

No one speaks as a police MATRON starts to lead Miranda to another room as other policemen separate Steven, Frankley, and Alfonso.

                    FERNANDEZ
                    (to matron)
    I'll be with you in a moment.

                    STEVEN
                    (doesn't know who to be angrier at, Fernandez or
                    Miranda)
    You won't find anything up there ... or
                    (motions knocking his head with his knuckles)
    up there either.

Miranda makes a mental note of this, glares at him.

                    FERNANDEZ
                    (to the policeman holding
                    Steven's arm)
    Examine him very carefully. Take your time, miss nothing, si?

POLICEMAN grins back.

TIME DISSOLVE TO:

Another office in the complex. Steven's clothes are disarrayed as he pays out his last $5,000 in U.S. currency to Fernandez.

                    FERNANDEZ
    You understand you are paying a fine for not filing a flight plan
    and for flying without lights, yes?

> STEVEN
>
> Yes, Colonel. I appreciate your not holding us any longer. Thank you.
>
> FERNANDEZ
> (counting the cash)
> Thank you, Mr. Green. After you sign this statement, you are free to go.

Steven nods, signs and leaves the office.

CUT TO:

HALLWAY OUTSIDE OFFICE - SAME

Steven shakes hands with Alfonso, reluctantly with Frankley, and motions Miranda to follow him.

FOLLOW HIM AS

He stalks off to the airline counters to find the next flight home to L.A.

EXT.

BEL AIR - GREEN MANSION - NEXT DAY

The SUN is just peeking over the horizon.

CUT TO:

INT. LIVING ROOM

Stretched out on couches, chairs, covered in blankets and sleeping fitfully are Itazumi, Mike, and Schwartz, whose toupee, not used to being left on all night has begun to peel back a bit from his scalp, exposing the lace underside.

ANGLE ON

Fat Detective, sipping coffee at his post by the telephone, while reading a late issue of Connoisseur from the coffee table.

CUT TO:

Leslie, in her bedroom, asleep. Beautiful as ever, but not resting well.

CUT TO: EXT. DAY

LAX INTERNATIONAL BUILDING - AEROMEXICO GATE

Steven and Miranda emerge along with other passengers streaming towards customs.

CUT TO: INT. CUSTOMS AREA

Steven and Miranda wait their turn, move slowly forward.

ANGLE ON MIRANDA

As her ditty bag is examined by CUSTOMS OFFICER. He smiles, motions her past him and she moves to exit to await Steven.

ANOTHER ANGLE

Steven in front of same Customs Officer;

                      OFFICER
    Anything to declare?

                      STEVEN
    No, nothing.

                    CUSTOMS OFFICER
    (examining his passport, punching numbers into computer)
    What was the purpose of your trip....business or pleasure?

				STEVEN
				(grimacing)
Pleasure.

				CUSTOMS OFFICER
			(looks up at him, checks photo)
You look familiar….have I see you before?

				STEVEN
				(nervous, remembering Col. Fernandez)
No ...

				CUSTOMS OFFICER
No baggage?

				STEVEN
Uh…private plane I was on went down in the ocean... lost everything.

				CUSTOMS OFFICER
I see... too bad. Well, computer checks you out....
				(hands back passport)

Steven starts to move on.

				CUSTOMS OFFICER (con't.)
I still think I know you from somewhere.

Looking back nervously, Steven hurries to join Miranda at the exit. They disappear through doors to street level.

CUT TO: EXT. DAY

STREET LEVEL OUTSIDE AEROMEXICO

Steven and Miranda head toward TAXI parked at curb. He opens door, they climb in. He turns to her:

                    STEVEN
          I don't even know where you live.

                    MIRANDA
          I'm staying at the Hollywood Roosevelt Hotel.

                    STEVEN
          Driver, did you hear that?

                    DRIVER
               (a recent refugee from somewhere)
          Da! Dhroshte!

Steven, whipped, just shakes his head, and is suddenly thrust back in his seat as the taxi ZOOMS away from the curb. He and Miranda are not communicating well.

                    MIRANDA
          So, what are you angry about, Steven? You wanted me, you
          got me. Do you always have a problem when your dreams
          come true?

He doesn't respond, just sinks deeper into his seat.

                    MIRANDA (con't.)
          Hmmm. I guess this is early withdrawal. Well, what we almost
          had was very special to me, and *I'll* always remember *you*.

CUT TO:

EXT. DAY - SAME

AERIAL SHOTS following taxi from LAX to Hollywood.

It's gonna be a hot one...the smog is a killer today.

CUT TO:

EXT. HOLLYWOOD BLVD. – Front of THE HOLLYWOOD ROOSEVELT HOTEL

DOORMAN opens cab door.

ANGLE OUT FROM INSIDE CAB

Miranda starts to get out. . Steven reaches in his pocket for a bill for the doorman, when he realizes he gave his last cash to Col. Fernandez. He grabs Miranda's arm;

                        STEVEN
     Wait a minute ... do you have any money I could borrow?

                        MIRANDA
     Why certainly, Steven, it's the least I can do.

She reaches in her bag, removes a couple of $20s and gives them to him.

                        STEVEN
     Thanks, I'll send you a check by messenger.

                        MIRANDA
     No, keep it, Steven. You'll need it more than I will.

She scoots out on his puzzled look.

BACK TO EXT.

Doorman slams door as Miranda disappears into hotel.

CUT TO:

Driver turns around to look at Steven.

STEVEN
120 St. Cloud Road in Bel-Air. You know how to get there?

DRIVER
Da! Dhroshte!

Steven is thrown backwards once more as the cab takes off.

ON: Steven, lost in thought, plays with his white hunter hat while trying to dream up his African story.

INTERCUT

DRIVER (ILLYA)
(looks in rearview mirror)
You a cowboy! I luff cowboys!

STEVEN
Huh? oh no..I'm not..just a businessman..
(he peers at I.D. card on dash)
Illya? Where you from?

ILLYA
From U.S.S.R...used to be, anyway.

STEVEN
(wants to be sure he heard right)
You used to be from U.S.S.R?

ILLYA
Nyet!...U.S.S R used to be U.S.S.R!

STEVEN
Oh ... right.

ILLYA
I be Amerikanski soon ... be just like you…wear big hat!

> STEVEN
> (feeling a bit overwhelmed)
> Yes...well, welcome to the U.S.

Goes back to his reverie.

> ILLYA
> Spasibo...where you come from?

> STEVEN
> Uh...originally? From New Jersey.

> ILLYA
> Nyet..nyet..

> STEVEN
> Oh, you mean now?
> (an opportunity to try out his story)
> Africa!

> ILLYA
> (regards him in mirror, whistles)
> You Amerikanskis...rich...can travel everywhere...I like!

> STEVEN
> It was business, actually. But everything went bad. I got on the wrong plane... my luggage went on without me. By the time I got there, the people who were to meet me were already in the bush...the guide I hired was a crook, we got lost, ran out of food and water, I was lucky to get back alive.

> ILLYA
> (rolls his eyes)
> Ay yay yay ... I thought I had big problem getting out of Russia! Hey, I tell you Russian joke. Make you feel better. My friend Boris goes to a bar, say to bartender, "Giff me three viskeys." Bartender pours viskey and say "Vot's 'dat under your arms?" Boris says "it's a cat, vot does it look like?" "Sure, a cat," say the bartender, "Under your other arm?" "A sack of manure," say Boris. Just now bartender sees a pistol in Boris's

belt. "Uh oh," say bartender. Boris drinks three viskeys, throws down sack of manure, pulls gun and fires three times into sack. Then Boris takes bite out of cat and throws it down. "What the hell is that?" say bartender. "I vant to be Amerikan," Boris say, "drink viskey, shoot shit, and eat pussy."

                  STEVEN
                 (winces)
Yes, it was awful! I'm so glad to be back. I can't wait to be home, see my wife ... forget about all this.

Steven slumps deeper in his seat, closes his eyes.

CUT TO:

INT.   BEL AIR - GREEN MANSION - SAME

Wake up time - Itazumi's on the tape recorder, replacing Fat Detective, who is stretched out on the floor asleep.

ANGLE OUTSIDE

Schwartz on the patio doing yoga exercises;

ANGLE INTO KITCHEN

Mike brewing coffee. Leslie is nowhere to be seen.

CUT TO:

EXT. - GREEN MANSION - SAME

Taxi pulls up to driveway, but can't enter due to profusion of vehicles blocking entry.

Parked at the front door is a huge MOVING VAN, the Monte Carlo, Itazumi's unmarked Squad Car, a cherry 57' PORSCHE SPEEDSTER painted racing green, 2 TV satellite VANS and 2 radio CARS from local radio stations.

216

ON STEVEN

Bewildered ... he pays Illya, exits cab, adjusts his white hunter's hat just so, walks up driveway and hesitantly goes through front door.

ANGLE INTO HOUSE

He is immediately brushed aside by THREE BURLY MEXICANS carrying out a large armoire. Odd... it looks a lot like the one he keeps his custom made shirts in.

HIS POV

Peeking around the corner from the entryway into the living room, he is stunned to see a crowd of strangers. Is he in the right house?

FOLLOW AS

He goes back out front door to check the address; the logo on the moving van looms at him:

C.U.: "Starving Mexican Students, Se Habla English".

CUT BACK TO TRUCK:

Through the open side doors of the truck he sees stacked up most of his furniture. What the hell is going on? Determined to find out, he squares his shoulders and stalks in. And all hell breaks loose!

CUT TO:

                          ESMERALDA
             Ohhh... meester!!! Pieded...Dios mio!!

INTERCUT:

Leslie turns around, spots Steven and SCREAMS:

                    LESLIE
       Darling!!
    (rushing over, she throws her arms around him, sobbing, then)
       Look, Rush Limbaugh, daddy's home!

The orange poodle emerges from under the coffee table, races, growling, towards Steven and from a full six feet away launches himself straight at his crotch – where he seizes whatever he can fit into his small mouth, bites down, and holds on. Steven whirls madly around, spinning Leslie off into a corner, trying to shake the dog off.

                    STEVEN
       Yoww…get him off!!

Leslie speeds over, forces the dog's mouth open, hands him over to Esmeralda.

They are immediately surrounded: Schwartz, Itazumi, Mike, Dottie, Fat Detective, Dianne and REPORTERS from the local TV and radio stations, thrusting microphones in his face while mini-cam lights blaze and cameras grind.

The din is awful, questions being thrown at him from all sides. Not only is he confused, but thoroughly scared as well. And for the first time in his life, he is speechless.

CUT TO:

Schwartz climbs up on dining room table, shouts above noise:

                    SCHWARTZ
       Everybody shut up, this is a police matter!!

The crowd ignores him.

                    SCHWARTZ
                    (yells)
       Find a chair and sit down before I arrest all of you.

CUT TO:

CROWD - begins to simmer down.

BACK TO SCHWARTZ:

                        SCHWARTZ
        You ... Green, sit there!
                  (points to couch)
        And the press...outside... Itazumi, get them outta here, I'll let you know when to bring em' back in!

CUT TO:

Itazumi nods and shepherds them outside, protesting all the way.

CUT TO:

Steven, seated on couch; Leslie crying softly, her arm around his shoulder. Dottie and Dianne look on warmly.

ANOTHER ANGLE

Just then, wandering into the room come Mr. & Mrs. Hashimoto and their interpreter, following a very tall, very thin aesthetic YOUNG MAN dressed all in black, with receding red hair pulled tightly into a ponytail. He carries a clipboard and a measuring tape. Oblivious to the action, he is measuring walls and jotting down notes.

CUT TO:

                        SCHWARTZ
        Now, everyone else but Mr. and Mrs. Green...out!
                  (to Hashimotos and group)
        And you too...you...decorators!

                        DOTTIE
                  (determined)
        I'm his mother... I'm not going anywhere!

                    DIANNE
                    (teary)
        And I'm his secretary...He needs me, I'm staying!

CUT TO:

                    SCHWARTZ
             (down off table, unwilling to
                take on any more angry females)
        Are you OK, Green?

ANGLE ON

Steven, in shock, nods.

ON SCHWARTZ

                    SCHWARTZ
        Well ... where the hell were you?

A crowd of defenders:

INTERCUT

                    DOTTIE
        Shame on you, Mr. Policeman.

                    DIANNE
        Leave him alone…don't you see he's very upset?

                    LESLIE
                    (to Steven)
        Darling, this is no time for you to have to answer
        questions...you look so tired.
                    (to Schwartz)
        Lieutenant, I'm not going to allow you to grill my husband like
        he's some criminal. Can't you see, he's been through a terrible
        ordeal...please come back later.

                    SCHWARTZ
            Hey, Mrs. Green...there are real criminals out there getting
            away with your money.

                    LESLIE
            That's unimportant. All that matters is that Steven is home.
                    (to Steven)
            Isn't it, darling?

CUT TO:

Steven nods cautiously...what the fuck is going on here?

C.U:

His eyes wander to the coffee table...on it, the LA Times;

INSERT

HEADLINE - "Industrialist Kidnapped," and his picture. That must be what alerted the guy at customs. Is that the best one they could find?

CUT TO:

Schwartz stands, utterly frustrated and marches to front door.

                    SCHWARTZ
                    (to Leslie and Steven)
            I'm right outside! I'll give you 15 minutes; then I want some
            answers!

He exits, slamming door, which opens immediately as FOUR more burly Mexicans, all Esmeralda's BROTHERS carry out Steven's bedroom set.

                    STEVEN
                    (trying to hang on, mumbling to himself)
            I got too much sun...this isn't real.

Steven is rushed by all the women in his life who love him; his mother, his secretary and his wife. They all hug him at the same time.

HIS REACTION

He may faint.

CUT TO:

EMPTY LIVING ROOM - LATER THAT EVENING

Even the pictures on the wall are gone. Steven and Leslie alone at last. He's propped up on pillows, leaning against the wall. Leslie puts another cold compress on his forehead.

INTERCUT

> STEVEN
> I was blindfolded the whole time...and left out in the sun.

> LESLIE
> Oh, darling...those animals...you poor thing. I feel so bad for you.

> STEVEN
> (looking around at the desolation)
> I never knew what hit me. The last thing I remember was going into the men's room at the airport...

> LESLIE
> I know, dear, you've said it... don't worry, I'll take care of you.

> STEVEN
> You're my best friend, Les. I love you and I'd be lost without you.

LESLIE
(patting his head)
Yes, that's true, dear. And I love *you* too, darling, so much, I want to be your widow.

STEVEN
(huh,? but too scared to ask)
Well…what did it cost to get me back? ...

LESLIE
Everything, I'm afraid.

STEVEN
(disbelieving
Everything...you don't mean...everything?

LESLIE
Yes, dear, but it was worth every cent. It's only money, and I'm not ever going to let you out of my sight again.

STEVEN
(in shock)
Oh...good..
(pause)
What about the business?

LESLIE
(soothing)
We managed to save it. We'll be working for nothing for the next ten years…but it doesn't matter, we have each other.

STEVEN
(adding it up)
Both houses... you mean the beach house too?

She nods.

STEVEN
The condo in Vail?

She nods again.

STEVEN
(apprehensive)
Not my Ferrari..

Another nod.

STEVEN
(a sob catches in his throat)
The Rolls too? My boat? I saw the furniture going out the door.

She doesn't even bother to nod.

STEVEN (cont.)
Your jewelry, too? Mine? My collection of Rolex's?

Leslie just looks sadly at the floor; then, brightly;

LESLIE
The Hashimotos didn't want our bikes, though. I guess they're too old. They are so sweet. We don't have to leave until tomorrow. We can spend our last night here... remember how we started with nothing?

He remembers...and sighs.

LESLIE (con't.)
Well, the good news is mom and dad. I know you think they never liked you all these years. I suppose it's true. They did want me to marry someone...<u>anyone</u> else. But they've come through for us.

STEVEN
(awakened from his thoughts)
Huh?

LESLIE
They're sending us some money- and guess what?

STEVEN
What?

LESLIE
I'm taking us away on a vacation…we haven't had one in years ... poor dear, you've been through a lot. Do you remember ... we wanted so much to go to Mexico on our honeymoon, but we didn't have the money?

He looks at her, unbelieving:

LESLIE (con't.)
Well, we still don't. But we're going anyway. We'll have some fun on the beach. And when we come back, we'll just start over again. And riding our bikes to work will be good for us too!

STEVEN
Wonderful… no time like the past.

He can only stare

LESLIE
I'll just run down to Western Union to pick up mom and dad's money. I'll be back in a little while, Darling. Don't move.

ON HIM

He nods weakly.

HIS POV:

Leslie exits.

BACK ON HIM

Hearing the SOUND of the cholomobile ROARING to life and peeling rubber out of the driveway, he jumps up.

FOLLOW HIM as he races through the empty house to the garage.

INT. GARAGE

POV:

In the corner; twin SCHWINNS.

He leaps on one, pushes with both feet out of the garage, picking up speed.

CUT TO:

MONTAGE

EXT. NIGHT

A mad, BREAKNECK RIDE as fast as he can pedal - through city streets from Bel-Air along Sunset Blvd. Through Hollywood, up Highland to Hollywood Blvd., to the HOLLYWOOD ROOSEVELT HOTEL.

INTERCUT VARIOUS SHOTS:

TAXI DRIVER purposely cuts him off, causing him to veer off Sunset, bumping over a curb and up a sloping lawn, crashing into a statue of a mailman delivering mail.

Speeding along Sunset in West Hollywood, a CITY BUS pins him between a row of parked cars, so that his handlebars sound like he's dragging a stick along a picket fence. He narrowly avoids being crushed by the bus by slowing down suddenly.

But so does the bus.

SPLAT!

As Steven thuds into the rear, it starts up again, releasing a vast cloud of black diesel fuel, most of which Steven inhales.

Coughing violently and covered in greasy diesel residue, he continues on, driven by anger and fear.

Finally reaching Highland Ave, he speeds through the light, turns left and makes it to Hollywood Blvd.

Turning right, the driver of a PARKED CAR opens his door, clipping his handlebars, throwing him over the top. Rolling to a stop, he looks up and is horrified to see HIS BIKE, clattering, skidding towards him, finally running him over.

                        DRIVER
                      (solicitous)
            Hey, you OK?

                        STEVEN
                (feeling around, checking his systems)
            I think so ...

                        DRIVER
                (suddenly angry and abusive)
            Then why the fuck don't you look where you're going?

                        STEVEN
            Huh? Me ? Why don't *I* look where I'm going? *You* hit me with your door!

                    DRIVER
Asshole! I'll show you how we take care of lawbreakers in Los
Angeles!

He yanks open his coat...revealing a shoulder holster!

Steven turns white through the film of street grime and diesel smoke, expecting to become LA's latest road kill, when the driver pulls out...a cell phone!

Steven pulls himself up, rights his bike, and woozily starts pedaling down Hollywood Blvd. In the B.G., he can hear the Korean driver shouting into his phone:

                    KOREAN DRIVER
        That's right officer ... no helmet!
CUT TO:

Bedraggled and weary, Steven pulls up to the front of the Hollywood Roosevelt Hotel.

POV THE DOORMAN

Steven leaves the bike with the surprised DOORMAN, dashes inside.

CUT TO:

INT. FRONT DESK

Steven, out of breath and sweaty.

INTERCUT

                    STEVEN
                (to desk clerk)
        Miranda Reed...what room is she in?

                    CLERK
          Is that i.e, or double e?

                    STEVEN
          Fucked if I know…

                    CLERK
                (consults his computer)
          I don't see anyone listed by that name, sir.

                    STEVEN
          Has to be...she's about
                (holds his palm shoulder high)
          this high...long blonde hair, green eyes, tiny nose ...
          (slows down as he starts to picture her beautiful body again).

                    CLERK
          Sir?

                    STEVEN
                (snaps out of it)
          Right...you know her?

                    CLERK
          I'm sorry, sir, but that's not an unusual description. Would you
          care to look in the bar?

                    STEVEN
          You're sure she's not a guest?

                    CLERK
          Quite sure, sir.

He turns away, discouraged, and heads for the street. Passing the bar, he decides, what the hell ... he'll take a look.

INT. BAR

He sticks his head in. lots of action. Wait a minute...is that HER?

He stalks in, gets closer, clearly it's not. Looks a lot like her though. THERE SHE IS! On the other side of the room...no, false alarm.

As he slowly spins around, there's easily half a dozen Miranda lookalikes scattered around the room, busily getting ahead.

At that moment, it begins to dawn on him just what has happened. Head hanging, he exits the hotel, lost on the sidewalk.

EXT. SIDEWALK

A PANHANDLER comes up to him.

                    PANHANDLER
           Spare some change?

                    STEVEN
                    (absently)
     It just cost me twenty million dollars to get laid.

PANHANDLER has heard some excuses in his time, but not this one. He moves on, pity in his eyes for Steven.

ON PANHANDLER

As he shuffles down sidewalk, he spots Steven's bike leaning against valet parking desk. Seeing doorman occupied with arriving limo and Steven lost in thought on sidewalk, panhandler takes bike and begins pedaling away.

ON STEVEN

                  STEVEN
                (to doorman)
        Where's my bike?

                  DOORMAN
  What bike? Do I know you...you got a receipt?

Broken all the way back to Private, and utterly dejected, Steven sadly begins walking back to Bel- Air.

CUT TO:

EXT. SAME NIGHT - LAX

Low clouds over the basin.

CUT TO:

PARKING AREA near Bradley Terminal.

HEADLIGHTS cut through the fog and gloom, illuminating a cherry '57 green Porsche Speedster.

SPOTLIGHT flashes the license plate.

CAMERA pulls back, sees the spotlight attached to Itazumi's car.

CUT TO:

INT. TERMINAL

OVERHEAD SHOT:

VERY CROWDED. Lots of PEOPLE milling about in front of various airline desks, standing in long lines, waiting for an available passenger agent.

CAMERA picks out a SMALL, ELDERLY BLONDE WOMAN wearing a kerchief on her head, carrying a large brown case, leaving Air France counter and disappearing into the crowd. She seems to resemble Dottie Green, Steven's mother.

CUT TO:

MOVING SIDEWALK to departure gates.

CAMERA travels along as if it were a passenger; STOPS suddenly to see from the rear a TALL BLOND WOMAN, whose pageboy flip looks like it could belong to DIANNE, Steven's secretary. Resting next to the woman is a large brown case.

CAMERA attempts to move forward to catch up, but is prevented by stationary PASSENGERS.

The woman leaves the moving sidewalk; goes through the gate to her Swissair flight. We've lost her!

CUT TO:

BOARDING AREA, VARIG AIRLINES

POV OUT THE WINDOW

A 747-B400 being loaded.

Several hundred PASSENGERS in various stages of boarding.

SPEAKERS announce:

 SPEAKERS
 Last call for Flight 2101 to Rio De Janeiro.

CUT TO:

INT. 747 FIRST CLASS CABIN

FIRST CLASS PASSENGERS settling in, putting articles in overhead compartments.

ATTENDANTS bringing drinks and newspapers.

ZOOM IN ON

A GORGEOUS WOMAN in 4A, next to the window.

MIRANDA sips white wine while leafing through the duty-free catalog. On the aisle seat next to her is her purse.

CAMERA becomes another passenger; stops at aisle seat:

                MIRANDA
          (looks up, a ten million dollar smile)
    Hi, nice to see you again.
            (removes her purse).

CAMERA pans up and down slightly as passenger nods "hello".

CAMERA pans up to open overhead compartment as passenger places overnight bag next to a LARGE BROWN CASE, slams compartment door closed.

CAMERA pans down as passenger takes seat next to Miranda.

CUT TO:

STOCK:

Varig 747 taking off into the night above Los Angeles.

CUT TO:

INT. LAX INTERNATIONAL BLDG.

Itazumi at Varig desk, scrutinizing passenger list, as several Varig OFFICIALS look on. She spots something...smiles.

CUT TO:

STOCK - DAY

The huge statue of Jesus atop Corcovado Mountain, above Ipanema, in Rio.

EXT. SAME

HEAVILY POPULATED BEACH

Signage advertises food and drink in PORTUGESE.

VARIOUS ANGLES

Umbrellas in profusion, CHILDREN splash in surf. A glorious day.

CUT TO:

1000 MM ZOOM LENS SHOT

In the distance, TWO WOMEN approach CAMERA, shimmering mirage-like because of the heat.

As they get closer, we see that like almost every other female on the beach, they're topless, and even from this far away, spectacular.

We know immediately one is Miranda, but the other?

As image slowly sharpens, LESLIE comes into focus.

STAY WITH THEM

They laugh together as they pass the camera, which pans to cover them from the rear. Miranda motions knocking her head with her knuckles. Both women laugh again.

                        MIRANDA
        That was definitely the most fun I've ever had with my clothes
        off.

                    LESLIE
          I don't think Steven would agree. I just happened to read in this
          morning's paper about this wealthy louse in Paris who's been
          cheating on his wife.

                    MIRANDA
          Paris, huh. I've never been to Paris.

                    LESLIE
          You'll love it.
                    (a big grin).

POV

Miranda and Leslie diminishing into crowd.

CUT TO:

EXT. ANOTHER BEACH

Jammed with VISITORS; this time all the signs are in ENGLISH.

CUT TO:

BOARDWALK, VENICE, CA

ANGLE ON

The purple and black Monte Carlo, parked with its rear pulled up behind a vendor's stand, its trunk open, packages of cosmetics stacked inside.

ANOTHER ANGLE

In front of the car is Steven, enthusiastically hawking his new line of skin care products to a small crowd of TOURISTS and SKATERS in thong bikinis.

BEHIND HIM

254

Large POSTERS feature a portrait of a beautiful woman, who looks a lot like Miranda in a jungle bikini, perched atop a huge bull Elephant.

BACK TO STEVEN

An attractive young woman has stepped up from the crowd. Steven is applying his new cream to her cheek.

        STEVEN
    You look lonely underneath that smile.

SLOW ZOOM PAST THEM TO POSTER - FREEZE IMAGE

FADE OUT.

www.ingramcontent.com/pod-product-compliance
Lightning Source LLC
Chambersburg PA
CBHW051402070526
44584CB00023B/3265